PORCH♥DOGS

PORCH♥DOGS

The Unmuzzled Truth About Men & Our Relationships with Them

Georgia Sullivan

Botchino!

Porch Dogs:
The Unmuzzled Truth about Men and Our Relationships with Them
Copyright © 2004 by Elaine Lee and Susan Norfleet Lee

Cover design by Teri K. Kwant

Illustrations and cover art by Herb Trimpe and James Sherman

Illustrations Copyright © 2004 by Botchino, Inc.

Library of Congress Control Number: 2001012345

Printed in the United States of America by
Vaughan Printing, Nashville, TN

ISBN: 0-9726863-0-4

Botchino Press
15365 Sierra Hwy
Santa Clarita, CA 91390

Acknowledgments

"I'll gladly pay you Tuesday for a hamburger today." - Wimpy

It's a wonderful thing to be able to make a living doing creative work... it's a remarkable thing to be able to work creatively with friends.

That said, my undying gratitude (and a groveling tug of the forelock) goes out to the following inspired artists and friends who helped bring this book into being: Brilliant illustrators Herb Trimpe and James Sherman not only supplied the book's fabulous and funny cartoons, but were willing to follow me out on a limb. Talented cover and logo designer, Teri Kwant, handled numerous changes with with a patience that was next to godliness. My editor, Augusta Ogden, was truly generous with her on-the-mark advice, much-needed moral support and her very black sense of humor. A tip of the Porch Dogs cap to Vicki and Steve Hickman. Thanks for the pawprints I used in the book's interior – and the fire hydrants I didn't. As for my imaginative, supportive and very funny publishers at Botchino Press, Elaine Lee and Susan Norfleet Lee - whose creative genius is surpassed only by their stunning physical beauty (They asked me to say that.) - I never could have done it with out you!

Now for the support team! A man I've never met, but truly love, Scott Nixon, programmed the Porch Dogs Quiz for the web site (www.porchdogs.com). My old high school bud, Mike McLendon, found Scott for me and convinced him this was a good idea. Brennan Lee Mulligan and Griffin Johnston gave me valuable teenage male input on the Men's Quiz that hopefully kept it from sounding "too girly." A grateful nod to web consultants Ray Lee and Laurie DiFalco, and to the only lawyer I know who does free phone consult, Melissa Marsh.

Acknowledgments

My most personal thanks must go to the close friends and family who saw me through the Porch Dogs years. My mother Dorothy (who was voted most talented in her high school class) gave me good genes, a sense of humor, determination and frequent grammatical corrections. She read the first (painfully long) drafts of this book and her comments were much appreciated. And most importantly, the lovable duo of Kristi Mordica and Richmond Johnston who kept me going with love, encouragement and cash. As soon as I sell some books, I'll buy you both something pretty.

TABLE OF CONTENTS

Introduction
If men are dogs, which breed is right for you?

We've heard it again and again: Men are dogs. A man in trouble with his wife is said to be in the doghouse, while a guy who chases women is a real dog. An aggressive man might be described as having a bark much worse than his bite. The man-as-dog concept permeates our popular culture. Men even refer to themselves as dogs. Snoop Dogg. Little Bow-Wow. Who let the dogs out? Put the big dogs on the field. Why would this idea be repeated so often, if there were no truth to it? And, why are dogs described as Man's Best Friend? Most importantly, what does choosing a dog have to do with choosing a mate?

In trying to answer these questions, let's first look at the very different ways that men and women go about choosing a dog. A man instinctively picks a dog that is like him... a partner with similar traits, a dog who will go hunting with him, or protect his home. A cowboy will pick a herding dog, an Australian Shepherd or a Queensland Heeler. If a man likes to hunt, he gets the hound or the sporting dog that was bred for his particular sport. He won't buy a dog on a whim any more than he'd propose to a woman on the first date.

Women choose differently. They believe in love at first sight. The big-eyed, flop-eared puppy on the pet adoption segment of the local news will get hundreds of inquiries from soft-hearted ladies who have called on impulse, ready to sign on for a lifetime commitment. Only later, when the darling puppy has become a hulking, designer-shoe eating, carpet-staining, china-breaking machine, will they learn the true cost of that hastily made commitment. Most women choose men the same way. They look, leap, and save the thinking for later, when it's much too late.

When I've asked my female friends why they chose the men they were involved with, they have tended to say things like, "He had such pretty blue eyes," or "His hair was so silky," or "He looked so handsome in his tux." See what I'm saying? Love at first sight. But the promise of that fateful first glance usually fails to live up to its potential. And whether you're in a singles bar or a dog pound, you'd do better to take a longer and much harder look before you leap into love. The fact is, if women would give as much thought to choosing the right guy as men do to choosing the right dog, they'd be happier, healthier and more content in their relationships.

So, where do we start? How do we begin to break our destructive patterns when it comes to choosing men? First, forget everything you've heard about man-caves, total honesty therapy, or rules that help you manipulate your way into a better relationship. Before we look at the men, we'll need to look at ourselves and at the three big mistakes women make when choosing a man.

Mistake #1

We look for a guy who will be EVERYTHING to us. And, we never find him. He doesn't exist. This is a job description that no human being is qualified to fill. There is no man alive who is capable of being all things to you. But taking the Porch Dogs quiz will help you find the type man who can be most of the things you need and want.

Mistake #2

We find a nice guy, then try to change him into a guy who will be EVERYTHING to us. This never works. People don't change easily. Of course, couples must compromise and learn to make small concessions for the sake of the relationship. But our basic temperament, our personalities, our likes and dis-likes are not likely to change. By having your man take the Porch Dogs quiz, you will learn which traits are responsive to change and which are the fixed traits of his "breed."

Mistake #3

We settle for the wrong guy. This usually happens once we've repeated the first two mistakes, time and time again, through a number of relationships, and still haven't found and/or created Mr. Perfect. Once we've gone for Mr. Wrong, we set about trying to change ourselves to suit him. This never works either.

It's a crime that the most popular save-your-relationship books on the market today advise women to alter themselves in order to win love. Surrender yourself! Play by the Rules! Lie about who you are and manipulate your way to happiness! Take my advice. Don't do it. You don't have to settle. You only need to start looking in the right place, for the right kind of man.

So, who is this book for? It's for the thirty-something Gen-Xer, looking for commitment after years of dealing with commitment-shy men. It's for the married woman who is weary of conflict and wants to better understand her mate. It's also for the man who is sick and tired of women who profess to love him, but who then proceed to try and change everything about him. It's even for the college student who wants to keep bad relationship habits from becoming habits in the first place. What's that? You say you aren't in a relationship and aren't really looking for one? You still have to work with men and deal with them on a daily basis. So, this book is for you, too.

Porch Dogs can help anyone have better relationships, in love or on the job, by forcing them to look at their relationships in a new way. And if even it doesn't help you find true love, you and your friends will have lots of fun (and more than a few laughs) trying to decide if your boss is a Bulldog or your boyfriend is a Basenji.

We visit the Pound

We Visit the Pound

The American Kennel Club lists 150 breeds in their registration statistics for the year 2002 and some breed books include as many as 200. As many of these breeds have overlapping traits, this book includes fewer breeds. I apologize if the exclusion of your favorite Havanese, Ibizan Hound, or Dandy Dinmont Terrier has caused you mental anguish. You'll just have to wait for the much-anticipated sequel: "Porch Dogs, The Rare Breeds."

In this first section of the book, we will visit the pound to learn about the many different breeds in the seven dog groups. You may browse the breeds now, or you may first want to turn to the back of the book and take our Porch Dogs Quiz. It's all so simple: Just score your quiz to find your matching breeds, then look up your best matches in the section covering each breed's dog group.

As you read through the breed descriptions, please keep in mind... while there are no bad dogs, some dogs make bad men. The very traits that make a Rottweiler a terrific guard dog may make the Rottweiler husband impossible to live with. And, yes, there can be some variation between individuals within a breed. It is possible to find a mellow Border Collie or a vicious Spaniel. I said possible, not probable. While there are rare exceptions to the rule, most men will be true to their breed.

Sporting Dogs – The Best of Sports!

SPORTING DOG MEN
(Includes Pointers, Setters, Retrievers and Spaniels)

Everybody loves a Sporting Dog Man! What's not to love? Devoted and good-natured, he's usually a family man, admired by all for his enthusiasm and love of life. If he is one of the retrievers, you can send him on endless trips to the corner for milk and he'll never protest. Setters and Pointers will enjoy nature hikes and sightseeing trips with the kids. The Spaniel Man is a charmer and loves socializing with friends. Though he may be gainfully employed, the Sporting Dog Man's real job is the weekend. That thing he does from nine to five simply supports his true calling... having fun with you!

At this point, you may be asking yourself, "What's the bad news?" There actually isn't much bad news when it comes to the Sporting Dog Man. Okay, he will be miserable if forced to stay indoors all day. When he's bored, he's fidgety and may tear the house apart looking for something to do. His "in the moment" personality and strong desire to please make the Sporting Man prone to spreading himself too thin. Because he's so friendly, undesirable types may latch onto him and be hard to shake. You'll have to watch out for what he may "drag into the yard." The flip side is that people hire him because they love him. You may find him in jobs where an engaging personality is a plus... among managers, teachers, salesmen, in the service industry, or the Peace Corps. He may be a talk show host, or a fundraiser for a good cause. Thanks to his love for his fellow humans, you may find him doing volunteer work... probably with kids.

But for the rare exception, don't expect a Donald Trump from this group. Though the Sporting Dog Man has great ability to focus on the job at hand, he is not a long-range planner. And money is not his main priority. Jimmy Carter, respected more for his kind heart and good works than his one term as president, seems like a Sporting Dog type. The late Jimmy Stewart may be another. Actually, a lot of guys named Jimmy fall into this group (except for Jimmy Conners, who is most likely a Terrier).

POINTER

When Pointer boys are old enough to talk, they will be talking about what they want to be when they grow up. Whatever that thing is, a Pointer man will be it with a vengeance. Whether it's carpentry, basketball, speed skating, fire-fighting, track and field, or operating heavy machinery, a Pointer man will dedicate himself to being the best at it. He'll research it, he'll practice it, he'll eat, sleep, and drink it. He will do it till he dies. He loves his work.

Head: Don't expect to take him to a party and have him join in a conversation about modern art or politics. When he talks, it will be about that thing he knows about, that thing he loves.

Heart: He's a simple, honest, straightforward, good, good man. And, he needs a simple, honest, straightforward, good woman. A woman who is sarcastic, critical, or condescending is the very worst match for him. Extremely sensitive, he'll pout when his feelings are hurt. If you snap at him, he'll be sure you don't love him. A sweet-tempered soul, he'll do best with a mate who is the same.

Family: Protective and warm with his children, he'll love to wrestle and play games with them. He'll never tire of giving piggyback rides. Best of all, he's tolerant of their imperfections. And if he has a child who wants to follow him in his work? He'll be in hog heaven!

Work: A physical guy, he's best with physical work to do. A Pointer might be happy as a carpenter, a surveyor, or a nature photographer. He loves the outdoors and any work that takes place there appeals to him. Many Pointers are athletes, as they have the stamina, talent, and dedication it takes to excel in this arena. A Pointer never minds the endless repetition it takes to perfect his skill.

Best Match with: Straightforward, sweet-natured, down-to-earth women.
Bad Breed for: Critics, blame-throwers, Sarcastic Sues.

GERMAN POINTER

A friend was recently regaling me with stories of her beautiful new beau. On and on she went about how athletic and handsome he was… how eager to please, how sensitive to her needs. Then the "but" slipped out. There was this one little thing that bothered her. He had this annoying habit of wrestling her. It was as if he would lose control of his senses and throw her to the ground out of sheer joy. Could it be a lack of exuberance control? "Ah Ha!" I said, knowingly, "He's a German Pointer!" Get used to the fact that he's going to wrestle you to the ground. Wrestling you to the ground, or onto the bed, or on the couch is just his way of saying that he needs to do something now!

Head: His restless mind makes for a restless body. He pops up during a rented video to run to the corner market. He bounces a tennis ball off the wall while you're reading. Like the child who constantly leans forward in the car to ask the back of your head, "Are we there yet?" the GP needs to get where he's going fast.

> FACT... The Internet is never fast enough. The microwave is wasting his time. The jerk in the car in front of him should pull over so he can go.

Heart: You're taking a romantic stroll through the park and he sees a pick-up game of basketball. In a flash, you're talking to yourself and he's setting a pick for some guy named Jam Daddy.

Family: Should kids enter the picture, you can sit back and watch him wrestle them. Remind him that infants have soft heads and their necks need to be supported. He'll be a super dad for rough and tumble kids, but you'll need to encourage him to be patient.

Work: He's one of those rare men who could be a professional athlete or a captain of industry. Whatever he chooses, the German Pointer is extremely busy. You can't overload him with work. He makes a schedule and sticks to it. As long as he's appreciated and happy in his work, he's the most productive guy you can have on your team.

Best match with: High energy, go-getter types.
Bad Breed for: The frail, the physically weak or touch sensitive.

CHESAPEAKE BAY RETRIEVER

I'm sure you've known one of those large families with several teenage boys who are hard to tell apart, always together, and who seem to exude a heady mix of optimism and testosterone. Well, meet the Retriever Brothers! You may remember them as the stars of the TV Western, "The Big Valley." Barbara Stanwick played the no-nonsense matriarch of the family, running the ranch with her three Retriever sons. The faithful and responsible older brother was Jared, the Labrador. Heath was the Golden Retriever, the charming youngest, loving and loved by everyone. And the Chesapeake? That would be Nick, the rough and ready middle son. Athletic and muscular, he's always the first to jump into the brawl. More stubborn than his "brothers" and much less accepting of strangers, Nick is a true macho man. A "shoot first, ask questions later" guy who defers to no man. Notice I said no man. If you were a fan of The Big Valley, you'll know that the matriarch ruled the roost. She was fair but firm, tough but feminine, loving, yet always able to keep her boys in line. If you want to have a happy and contented life with a Chesapeake Bay Retriever, you must become Victoria Barkley.

Head: Like his TV counterpart, the Chesapeake man is territorial and highly competitive. Challenge him to do something and, by God, he'll do it. Just make sure you don't bet against him! A

Sporting Dogs

Chesapeake man has an iron will that often makes up for short comings in other areas.

Heart: Once he loves you, he'll love you forever. But you must be honest with him. Women who play emotional games don't do well with this retriever. Because he's protective and possessive, making him jealous is a bad idea. Flirting with an unsuspecting man at a party could mean a bloody nose for the poor soul.

Family: Like his two brothers, he loves children, but is the least likely of the retrievers to take guff from a mouthy kid. He'll demand respect and, though he'll be a real teddy bear with his youngsters, his older male children may run into problems with him once they're at the "challenge authority" age.

Work: Not made for the corporate, nine-to-five world, a Chesapeake just won't be happy indoors. You may find him working with his hands, driving heavy machinery, running a ranch or construction crew. As he's dedicated and hard working, he will support his family nicely, but doesn't like frill or excess. He will not want to see his hard-earned money spent carelessly.

Best Match with: Victoria Barkley types.
Bad Breed for: Frivolous women, wimps, and flirts.

GOLDEN RETRIEVER

I walked into a corner deli, in upstate NY, where a handsome, sweet and engaging young man greeted me from behind the counter. After we chatted for a moment, I looked into his smiling face and asked, "If you were a dog, what kind of dog would you be?" The young man thought for a moment and robustly replied, "Golden Retriever!" If he had had a tail, it would've been wagging. Just like Heath, the gorgeous, golden, youngest son in "The Big Valley" (see Chesapeake Retriever), he's full of life and exuberance, joy and positive energy. He's everybody's buddy and many women's dream guy. What's not to like? He's cute and cuddly, cheerful and trusting. He's fun to date and easy to be married to. No great mood swings, no temper tantrums. He's consistent and cooperative... a confident, robust, warmhearted hunk.

Head: Oh, all right. There is one little negative. Like his buddy, the Irish Setter, our Golden boy is a bit distractable. Though less extreme than the Irish, your Golden may sometimes have to be reminded that he needs to stay on course.

Heart: This man likes to hug. He likes to hug, he likes to slap backs, he likes to keep his arm around you, he likes to ruffle children's hair. You may have to remind him gently that not everyone thinks one foot of personal space is enough... or that some parents aren't comfortable with the sight of their infant being tossed into the air by men they don't know.

Family: That's right. A Golden Man loves kids. He loves his kids, your kids, everybody's kids. He's an involved and caring parent. He'll happily haul children around, play games with them, nurse them when they're sick, or fall asleep under a pile of them. No one with a Golden dad has ever wound up in therapy complaining about a lack of love in the family.

Work: Golden Men are naturals in service-oriented jobs. You might find him working as a physical rehabilitation therapist. He's the guy leading a group of fourth graders on a nature hike through the State Park. Or, he's teaching fourth grade. (He's the teacher all the kids want.) If he's selling kitchen appliances at Sears, he'll sell a lot of appliances. You'd want to buy that microwave just to see him smile. He doesn't so much follow his bliss, as create bliss wherever he goes.

Best Match with: Most people
Bad Breed for: Elitists, hug haters, personal space fanatics

LABRADOR RETRIEVER

The best way to understand the Labrador Retriever is by comparing him to the Golden and Chesapeake, his closest kin. Less aggressive than the Chesapeake, more focused than the Golden, our Lab is the older, responsible, square-jawed brother (see Chesapeake Retriever). He's the man your mother wants you to marry. Whether he's running a football toward the goal posts, or dressed in his tux for a formal dance, the Lab is completely masculine. Both elegant and vigorous, he's the guy others refer to as "a man of character." Every bit as lovable as the Golden, the Lab is more stable and less likely to be distracted. He is sturdy, determined, powerful and self-willed. Well-built and athletic, he's never thick-necked or muscle-bound.

Head: The Labrador has the substance and soundness of mind to work for hours under difficult conditions, and the character and quality to come out on top, no matter what profession he chooses.

Heart: He'll seem as though he's always got a handle on things, but he needs to know that you care. Giving him a back rub, or planning a candlelight dinner, will tell him that you really appreciate him.

Family: Though he is strong-willed, the Lab is also friendly, good-tempered, and kind. This sweet and gentle temperament makes him a dream companion, caring lover, and doting dad.

Work: This is a man you can count on. He won't fall apart and he'll never drop the ball. Though he's very alert, learns quickly and pays close attention to details, he's not likely to be a Mensa member. The Lab's stable temperament makes him suitable for a variety of pursuits from law enforcement to litigation, UPS to FBI. In business, he'll be tough, but fair-minded. He won't engage in unethical business practices or try to cheat the IRS. Whatever he does, the Lab will do it well.

Best Match with: Almost anyone with a pulse.
Bad Breed for: Those who can never be pleased. (He'll try to please you till he dies.)

ENGLISH SETTER

Just down the street from the Retrievers live their good pals, the Setter boys... English, Gordon, and Irish. The most calm and stable of the Setters is the English. He's quiet without being shy, friendly, but never overbearing, graceful and well mannered, without being elitist. Very astute, he's that rare man who reads people well, yet still manages to enjoy their company. Though some find him overly anxious to please, he is, at the same time, easygoing and secure. "A paradox," you say? Not at all. Just the perfect blending of many admirable qualities. If you could mix Hugh Grant and Kevin Costner in equal parts, you might end up with an English Setter Man. Extremely adaptable, he won't mind changing to suit the needs of his companion. Of course, he has needs of his own. He definitely needs room. Even if he works in the city, he'll want to live in the suburbs. If an English can afford it, he'll have a country home. He loves the outdoors, but prefers long walks in the woods to activities like cliff climbing or skiing. He'd rather spend a leisurely day on the golf course than an exhausting hour in a handball court.

Head: Some rigid souls may be annoyed, because he rarely takes a firm stand. "If you can see everyone's point, what's yours?" But, that's not our Englishman's problem. If he's received new information, he sees no reason why he shouldn't take it under consideration.

Heart: Not a good choice for women who want a decisive, take-charge guy. And, because he's so in tune with his surroundings, he won't do well with screamers and "get out your anger" types. He should never marry into a large, loud Italian family, or a passive-aggressive family that loves to exchange sarcastic barbs.

Since your Englishman's more concerned with people than he is with things, he can be oblivious to the state of his house and his personal appearance. You'll have to straighten his tie, turn down his collar, and remind him it's time to visit the barber.

Family: Emotionally available and always ready for family time, the English makes a lovely husband and father. Though he's watchful, he's never over-protective and won't bully his kids. He'll talk to you about his feelings and yours. Though he enjoys the company of others, he's happy to relax at home with you.

Work: His ability to read people makes him a perfect candidate for judge, but you should watch to make sure his job doesn't sour his natural affection for humankind. He may be happier working as a mediator. The English Setter man might teach ethics at a college, sit on the school board, or be the mayor of a small town. He has more than a bit of Sheriff Andy Taylor in him.

Best Match with: Affectionate, casual women.
Bad Breed for: Women who need a lot of looking after, screamers, obsessive cleaners.

GORDON SETTER

The Gordon man takes the same role in the Setter family that the Chesapeake holds in the Retriever clan. He's the most athletic, is powerfully muscled and full of masculine vigor. He prefers the outdoors to the indoors. The Gordon takes longer to warm up to strangers than his brothers, the English and Irish boys. He's more dominant and aggressive with other men. He's a little bossier, too, though he stops far short of being a control freak. He can be possessive, but isn't always so. Socially, the Gordon's just as comfortable clowning it up at a backyard barbecue, as he is waltzing with the CEO's wife at an elegant fundraiser. But he's no gad-about or social butterfly. He'd rather make his off-time a family affair. Encourage him to interact with the larger community, as he's the kind of man who can become so content with his family that he feels no need for outsiders.

Heart: If he's feeling sad or down on himself, he won't like sharing you with anyone else. When things are going well, he's less needy of attention. Since he's emotionally open with his partner, a rare quality in such a manly man, you'll be able to work through any problems. He's always happy to talk it out.

Head: He doesn't have the attention span problems that you'll find with his bright but irresponsible Irish sibling. He's dependable, tireless and methodical. His job is definitely not his first priority. That would be his kids.

Family: He'd rather spend time with his children than any other people on earth. How protective he is with his children will depend on his mood. When he's feeling insecure, he'll be more likely to see danger around every corner. You can help him by explaining that kids need space to develop independence.

Work: The Gordon won't be comfortable stuck in an office cubicle. He'll be a surveyor, or run a well-drilling business. He may be a traveling salesman, or work for the parks department or the forestry service. He could be part of an environmental effort to teach third-world farmers about sustainable agriculture. This man works well in a partnership, though he'll be the partner looking for problems out in the field, never the guy keeping accounts on the computer.

Best Match with: Physically active, social women.
Bad Breed for: The emotionally repressed, hermits.

IRISH SETTER

Excitable, impulsive and highly distractable, the Irish Setter man is the least focused of the Setters, perhaps of the entire Sporting group. If he's a student, he's probably changed his college major five or six times. If he's out working, he gets bored and quits the job just about the same time he gets good at it. The phrase "Jack of all trades, master of none" really applies to this Setter. This is a man who must be trained. Having said that... good luck! It will take the patience of a saint to whip this guy into husband material. Don't let him do the grocery shopping without a list, unless you want to dine on beer, frozen dinners and music CDs for the next week. Thanks to his rollicking, high-on-life persona, this walking celebration has no problem attracting friends and admirers. But his motto might be: "Great date, iffy husband."

> **IS YOUR EX AN IRISH?**
> Don't expect much in the way of child support. He's not an evil guy, it just doesn't occur to him that his child might have financial needs. Since his kids are sure to love him like a god, try to keep your anger in check.

Head: He screws up so often, you could be tempted to conclude that the Irish Setter man is less than bright. You'd be dead wrong. In fact, he's quite intelligent, the brainiest of the Setter Clan. His problem stems from over-exuberance and from having the shortest of attention spans. If you want to help him, encourage him to make lists. Then, encourage him to read the lists. Then, remind him again.

Heart: You may need to remind him that not everyone loves puns and practical jokes the way he does. And he's the master of the "big fish" story. Explain that, while enthusiasm is an admirable quality, some experiences don't deserve "Isn't it incredible" status.

Family: Though he'll love his kids, he's not a great dad for very young children. They're too much work and he doesn't know what to do with them. He may get distracted and leave the amusement park without the kid! Once they're old enough to memorize the phone number, or find their own way home, things will be fine.

Work: The perfect job description for an Irish Setter is "Idea Man." He comes up with ideas, others execute them, thus taking advantage of his quick mind, while making allowances for his short attention span. The worst case scenario? Your Irish Setter is self-employed, starts a million projects, finishes nothing, loses the checks on the way to the bank, and tax time is a trip to Hell. That's assuming he even bothers to file! April's such a beautiful month! Who can sit at a table with a calculator when there are flowers to smell and puddles to skip through?

Best Match with: Those with good humor and a good memory.
Bad Breed for: Daddy's girls.

BRITTANY SPANIEL

He likes your family. He likes your friends. He likes your co-workers, your kids from a previous family, your ex-husband, your ex-husband's family, and your creepy neighbor Ned who lives across the street and watches you with binoculars. He invites Ned over for barbecues. A Brittany man likes everyone indiscriminately. Most importantly, he loves you. He loves, loves, loves you. You wake to find him staring at you. He calls you at work, several times a day, just to say he misses you. He insists on holding your hand in August when you're sweaty and hot and the thought of closeness to another human makes you want to kill yourself. "I need my space" will not work with him.

Head: As his mind is very active, his need to be with you may become obsessive. Keep him busy. If you need a day away from him, tell him you'll make sandwiches while he calls his buddies over for a game of softball. If you need time alone in the house, buy him season tickets to... anything.

Heart: The Britt's incredible enthusiasm can lead to disappointment when experience doesn't live up to expectation. He'll be in an ecstatic frenzy for weeks before Christmas, preparing for the big day, buying the "perfect" gifts and building up a holiday head of steam.

> If you're a woman who worries about break-ins, you'll have to buy a security system. This man is too trusting to offer much in the way of protection.

35

But, Christmas Day may be a letdown that will plunge him into days of depression. If little Timmy refuses to play with that customized Tonka Truck, he could go straight to bed and sleep until New Year's Eve. You can help by remembering to give him credit for the many things he does for you.

Family: If you have kids, alone time won't be a problem. The only person who enjoys play more than a child is a Brittany. Send them out to the amusement park while you dive into that bestseller!

Work: If you're a boss, this is the guy you want for your "number two" man. He's completely loyal and would never betray you or even think of trying to steal your job. He's also capable, enthusiastic, and he comes in with a new idea every day.

Best Match with: Team players. Go-with-the-flow gals.
Bad Breed for: Sedentary women, sad sacks, doom-sayers.

COCKER SPANIEL

See him work the room? Moving from group to group, kissing the women, slapping guys on the back, telling jokes, doling out compliments? He's energetic, he's positive, he's happy, he's fun, with a great sense of humor and charm to spare. The Cocker Spaniel man is a real party animal. Not a breed for wallflowers and stay-at-home women, this guy wants to go out on the town! He's a great dancer and, if you're married to him, he'll dance with all your friends who came to the party alone, and with those whose husbands refuse to dance with them. He enjoys his creature comforts, so forget that weekend roughing it in the wilderness.

Heart: Cocker men hate confrontation. He won't fight with you, but if he's unhappy, he may blindside you with passive-aggressive digs about your weight or your hair or your friends. Since he can't say "Honey, I'm miserable because you've gained forty pounds," he'll say, "Wow! I've never known a woman who could put away so many donuts."

> The worst thing you can do to this man is let yourself go. He wants his pretty wife or girlfriend to stay that way. So, stick to that diet and join the nearest gym.

Head: In his mind, he's still twenty years old. Whine about your hot flashes and you'll soon notice his tail wags a little less frequently. He probably won't leave you, he'll just be miserable. This man needs a playmate. So, if you notice he is no longer the happy-go-lucky guy you fell for? It's probably you, not him. Get your act together or set him free. A miserable Cocker is an affront to nature.

Family: Cocker make great dads. He loves kids and will probably want them. Remember, he's a big kid himself! But if your financial situation is not a good one, please put off having a family until things are more stable. If your Cocker is spending his "dad" time working three jobs just to support you, he won't be as much fun when its time for fun. Relentless drudgery is definitely not his thing.

Work: Look for a Cocker in fields that require personality and charisma. He may be a cruise director, travel agent, entertainer, or restaurateur. If he owns a restaurant or club, he'll be there every night, greeting people at the door. Full of natural curiosity, he'll enjoy any job that requires learning something new, or meeting someone new, every day. Some of this breed can be found in "flushing and retrieving" jobs, such as corporate headhunting and film casting.

Best Match with: Happy, funny, young-at-heart women.
Bad Breed for: Party poopers, domineering women, agoraphobics.

SPRINGER SPANIEL

The quintessential Good Time Charlie, Springer men are full of enthusiasm and high-spirited affection. He will fill your house with flowers, play the clown, do almost anything if it will bring you cheer. Every day is Valentine's Day with a Springer. There's only one person who can rain on his one-man happiness parade. You. He may pick up anxiety from you. When you worry, he worries. He never tires of saying, "we like this" or "we believe that" and will have to be reminded that the two of you are individuals. You'll probably tap him on the shoulder more than once to let him know that he's the one who likes oatmeal, not you. But he doesn't mean to step on your toes. He just loves being part of "we." Let him know early in the relationship that there will be times you will want to go somewhere by yourself, and that it doesn't mean you don't love him. Setting the guidelines early is the only way to keep him secure and content.

Heart: Because he's so sensitive to you, he'll know when you're pulling away or feeling the need for more space. This doesn't mean he'll be able to give it to you. A Springer Man has a hard time giving you space, especially when he's already feeling insecure about the relationship.

Head: The Springer enjoys challenges. When a problem rears its ugly head, he rises to the occasion. If it rains on the camping trip, that's just great. It will teach him something valuable. He's not the type to cut and run when the going gets tough and is not likely to spring the "I want a divorce" line on you. If things aren't great in the relationship, he'll try everything he can think of to make it better.

Family: A Springer dad is wonderful with his kids because he has the ability to enter into their world. He talks like a kid, walks like a kid, plays like a kid, and still manages to be a responsible dad. His only problem in the daddy department will appear when the kids begin going through their independent stage. Again, you'll find yourself having the "it's nothing personal" conversation with him.

Work: The Springer man follows his bliss and is "Mr. Intense" in the workplace. The perfect employee, he's loyal, energetic, enthusiastic and perpetually positive. But your Springer will be happier if he's never involved in the hiring and firing department. He'll want to hire everybody and fire no one. He's unlikely to be a boss. Very much a mainstream guy, he probably won't be an inventor or an entrepreneur. Though he's no visionary, he has the ability to appreciate the vision of another and will work very hard for something, or someone, he believes in.

Best Match with: Another 1/2 of a "we", extroverts.
Bad Breed for: The easily embarrassed, the anxious, space-needers.

VIZSLA

If your big complaint about men is that they are oblivious to everything except the location of the TV remote, we have one word for you: Vizsla. I ran into my Vizsla friend, George, the other day. After we exchanged hugs, the first thing he said to me was, "I love what you've done with your hair!" My stylist had highlighted my hair weeks earlier. Subtle highlights. The kind even your best girlfriend doesn't notice. George the Vizsla noticed. A Vizsla man will notice everything. He'll notice you're wearing new earrings, changed your perfume, or plucked your eyebrows. Before you get too excited, he'll also notice you've put on a few pounds, missed your annual teeth cleaning or neglected to vacuum. He is, to put it mildly, a very alert fellow. The Vizsla needs physical activity, so an active, athletic partner is his best match. Before you volunteer to go on that jogging date, you might want cross-train for a few months ahead of time. This man has stamina! Your romantic little jogging adventure could end with you heaving and wheezing, while he trots in place looking down on you with mild annoyance. Not sexy.

Heart: If sex doesn't mean much to you and you're only in your twenties, do not pair up with a Vizsla. He'll keep his body and his sex drive well into his senior years and will hate it if you don't. He won't mellow with age. You'll be knitting by the hearth and he'll be out on the sailboat with Becky, the twenty-year-old cashier from Home Depot.

Head: Help him avoid chaotic situations, as he may have trouble screening out noise and other stimuli. This could cause him to become overly anxious. Remind him that not every insight he has should be shared.

Family: The Vizsla dad gets my five star rating. He'll never try to mold his children to his likeness. He'll recognize the child's innate abilities and temperament and will support and nurture them as individuals. If his kids are athletes, he'll toss the ball with them. If he sees he has fathered a Prima Ballerina, he'll supply the slippers and lessons. If his child has a high IQ, he'll fill the house with computers and books. He'll also help his child overcome areas of weakness, tutoring the athlete in math, or schlepping his little Einstein to karate class.

> If he lives in the city, he'll be one of those quick thinking, fast-reacting, slightly jumpy guys who is aware of every person on your subway car and has mentally tagged which ones could be a problem, so that he can steer you out of harm's way.

Work: With his ability to take in and analyze huge amounts of information, he'd make a great mission control specialist for NASA. You might find him running focus groups for the ad industry, working as a political campaign coordinator, or a hospital administrator. Any job that combines the ability to process information with the ability to see into people's souls will be appropriate for the Vizsla.

Best Match with: Active MENSA members and unusually smart sex kittens
Bad Breed for: Couch potatoes, hot tempers, frigid partners.

WEIMARANER

Talk about stamina! If the Vizsla man likes sex often, the Weimaraner man likes marathon sex. Forget quickies and fake orgasms, because really! How many times can you fake an orgasm? And don't think that telling him you're not in the mood will end the conversation. A Weim loves nothing more than a challenge. He'll woo you, court you, put on sexy music, or a naughty video. If that doesn't work, he might guilt you, whine, or pout. He really tries to get his way. The bold and impetuous nature that attracted you in the beginning, can quickly morph into stubborn and bullheaded once you're involved. If you think you can win the battle of the wills, make sure your will is iron. Anything short of aerobics instructors, marathon runners, professional soccer players, or Olympic track athletes, will have a hard time keeping up with a Weim. You're in luck if he's a professional athlete, as he'll have a place to put his amazing energy. If he didn't make the cut, start working out now. If you can't keep up with him, he'll find someone who can.

Head: He's really smart. Remind yourself that smart doesn't mean cooperative. A Weimaraner man would much rather do things his way, even if his way is clearly not the good way. If he feels pushed or nagged, he'll turn and run in the other direction.

Heart: He's not going to be all warm and fuzzy with strangers. This man goes with his gut, and if his instincts tell him someone's questionable, you'll never convince him otherwise.

Family: A Weim can make an acceptable dad, but you'll have to remind him that babies aren't footballs. Also, insist on safety helmets and suggest that three-year-olds shouldn't be allowed to ride horses by themselves.

Work: He puts his heart, soul, and every ounce of physical effort into the job at hand. Weimaraners tend to excel in two fields of endeavor: business and sports. In business he's the company star, respected by his colleagues. (I said respected, not loved.) If you work for him, never make excuses for failure. This man hates whining, so just take responsibility and try not to do it twice. In sports, the Weim is best in solo competition, where he'll be allowed his star status. In games like soccer and basket-ball, that require cooperation between team members, he'll have to constantly be reminded to pass the ball.

Best Match with: Super-athletes, diplomats.
Bad Breed for: Pushovers, slugs, nags.

WIREHAIRED POINTING GRIFFON

Square-jawed, strong, and forceful, the WPG man is also high-strung and edgy. Think John Wayne on a coffee jag. And while life with this man will certainly be exciting, it may also be a trial. Behind the Griffon man's bravado, there may lurk a sack-full of insecurities. He struggles with his sensitive nature and desire to please on the one hand, and his need for independence on the other. Thanks to this inner struggle, your WPG can be unpredictable and, in some cases, more than a little unstable. Because he's smart, he'll do well at his chosen profession, though he probably won't rise to the highest rank. He's just not as cutthroat as some of his peers and that may keep him one or two rungs from the top of the success ladder. Reminding him that you didn't marry a CEO might make it easier for him to handle this perceived shortcoming.

Heart: The macho type of Griffon man is more comfortable with strangers than with family. At the same time, he tends to get overwrought around strangers and can work himself into quite a spin. He seems to pick up on the energy of others and can't screen out their negative emotions. On the other hand, a Griffon who has learned to be comfortable with himself is a treasure. A dependable and loving family man with a great (and usually self-deprecating) sense of humor.

Head: Anything new or novel can be overwhelming for a Griffon. Think you'd like to try that new chicken dish? Think again. The anguish that cream sauce will cause him isn't worth it.

Family: Griffon men tend to be no-nonsense dads. "Because I said so!" is an oft-repeated phrase. He'll also treat his kids like small adults. You may hear him say to his five-year-old, "Don't you know better than that?" Of course, the five-year-old doesn't know better. He's five years old. The good news is, once your kids are old enough to debate with him, he may actually listen to them.

Work: The perfect job for this man? Looking for bugs in the system. Or auditing books for signs of tax evasion. Or creating worst-case scenarios. Or scanning radar screens for the blip that means "incoming enemy missiles." He will be relentless in his dedication. If there's an enemy out there, he will, by God, find him. He might be a crusader who believes everybody needs to be investigated. He may be a member of a radical environmental group. He could be Ken Starr. At his best, he's a highly effective worker. At his worst, he's a conspiracy nut.

Best Match with: Earth Mothers and other very calm, nurturing women.
Bad Breed for: Nervous or paranoid partners, hard-drivers.

He ain't Nothin' but a Hound Dawg

HOUND MEN

He's a good ol' boy, out carousing with his bowling buddies after the big tournament. He's also the inspired loner, ready to follow his inner voice to a place "no man has gone before." Confusing? Then let me clear things up for you. Men of the Hound group come in two very different flavors, the Scent Hounds and the Sight Hounds. Though different in many respects, both types are more independent and less excitable than men of the Sporting Dog Group. Both Scent Hounds and Sight Hounds are hard to keep at home.

Elvis Presley cruising around Memphis, his Cadillac packed with friends, is a perfect example of the Scent Hound type. Very social, Scent Hounds often travel and work in packs. When not out in the yard with a ball, you may find this guy in a sports bar watching the game with his pals. At his best, he's boyish, boisterous, intensely masculine and utterly charming, with a voice you can hear halfway across the next state. There is a negative type of Scent Hound that can be dangerous in packs. "If you're not pack, you're prey" is the mentality. You might see these guys driving past a lone woman, howling from their car windows.

As with the Scent Hound, your Sight Hound may spend most of his time out of your sight. But you won't lose him to the pack and you won't find him down at the local pub, howling with his buddies. This man is more likely to be lost in his work. Sight Hounds are visionaries, artists, composers, physicists, philosophers, inventors, mountain climbers and radical priests... anyone who marches to the beat of his own and very different drum. A woman who loves a Sight Hound will often be heard to say, "I fell in love with his work"... or his talent, or his politics, or his mind. This kind of partnership isn't always easy. In the last scene of Casablanca, when Ingrid Bergman's character steps onto that plane with Victor Lazlo, leaving Humphrey Bogart behind, she is choosing to follow her Sight Hound's vision, even though it means giving up romantic love.

AFGHAN HOUND

Look at that incredible man brooding in the corner of the coffee bar, several empty espresso cups on the table before him, his long, flowing hair falling provocatively over one eye. He stretches… his black leather pants cling tightly to his lean, muscular legs. He's so tortured, so beautiful, so deep in thought. So deep. (Re: the word "deep." A swimming pool can be deep but if it's not filled with water, it's pretty useless.)

If you think that you can relieve his pain, plumb his psyche, make him add color to his wardrobe… or if you're picturing yourself driving to the PTA meeting with Mr. Afghan in your minivan, my advice to you is GET OVER IT! If you start talking about "his and hers" anything, he will change his name and move to Bolivia. If you dote on him, pamper him, spoil him and lose your identity, he will let you do it… then toss you in the trash like outdated milk.

Head: This man lives in his own head and roomy though it may be, he will rarely let you in. You'll never know what he's thinking, which in many cases may be a blessing. He will constantly forget anniversaries, birthdays, and dinner party invitations.

Heart: There is some good news here. He's beautiful, predictable, and won't pull any macho trips on you. He won't get into bar fights and he won't hit you. He's not terribly fussy about his things and he won't throw a fit because you borrowed his CD's. If you're independent and know your own worth, or are completely self-involved, this could actually work out for you.

Family: If you want your kids to spend the bulk of their young adulthood in therapy, go for it. It's probably best to find other ways to deal with your ticking biological clock. Start with a plant and work your way up to a puppy.

Work: The Afghan man is most often found in solitary work. He's the kind of guy who circumnavigates the world by himself... in a kayak... maybe a hot air balloon. He may also be a writer, painter, philosopher, or social critic. That new book called "Zen Koans Composed While Kayaking the Great Water"? He wrote that book.

Best Match with: Career women, artists, non-needies.
Bad Breed for: The project-minded, empty vessels, masochists.

BASSET HOUND

If your idea of heaven is a sweet, easy-going guy loudly snoring on the couch, surrounded by kids and clutter, have we got a guy for you! The Basset Hound man gives the term "laid-back" a whole new meaning. He also gives new meaning to the word "slob." He's not going to do the dishes, he's not going to do the laundry, he's not going to sweep the floor or make the bed. If you're the kind of woman who enjoys housework, and by that I mean all the housework, life with a Basset might be your bliss. The Basset man enjoys the company of his male friends and will schedule regular weekly pack outings for bowling, poker, ball games or hunting.

Heart: At your summer party, he will not be in the kitchen chatting with the girls. He'll be out on the patio flipping burgers, jawin' with the guys. It's not that he doesn't like women, he just fears being trapped in a conversation where someone forces him to reveal something intimate. He saves that side of himself for you. At a gathering, he's more comfortable discussing fishing lures, his beer collection and NASCAR.

Small Irritant... Basset Men are notorious food stealers. He will pick off your plate, he will take the last piece of pie, he will eat your French Fries when you're not looking. He will also put the empty milk carton back in the fridge after he's finished it off.

Head: You cannot boss this man at all. If you yell and scream, threaten or push, he'll pretend he can't hear you and leave to go golfing. The only way to get your way with him is to bribe him. Offer to cook his favorite meal, get him tickets to a play-off game, promise him a night of wild sex. Only then will you get your garbage disposal fixed.

Family: This is the dad who takes all the neighborhood kids hiking and accompanies them on field trips. Any woman partnered with this man should encourage these outings, as this will be her only vacation from picking up after him. When a Basset meets his soul mate, he'll never stray. In his eyes you will be Sophia Loren, Vivica Fox and Ashley Judd all rolled into one. For some women, that's worth all the vacuuming in the world!

Work: Whatever this man does for a living, he does it within a pack. He's extremely hardy and has great endurance. He may work for an organization that searches for missing children. He may be a professional bounty hunter. Unfortunately, you might also find him working for a collections agency. Just hope he doesn't get your name on his list.

> The Basset will not get a lot of promotions and will never blow his own horn. If you want to retire comfortably, start socking away a bit of his paycheck every week.

Best Match with: Understanding gals and happy homemakers.
Bad Breed for: Shrill chicks, clean freaks, and brow-beaters.

BEAGLE

Looking for a Beagle man? First, find an event where unruly men gather in large numbers. The Dallas Cowboy Cheerleader try-outs, a strip club, or a pro wrestling match. Second, locate the loudest and most annoying group of men. Third, approach the group and dare one of them to do something insane. The one who does it is a Beagle. He's the kid who runs naked though the gym during the high school pep rally. He will strap himself to anything with wheels and let other guys push him down steep inclines. He's the dude in the horror movie who goes to check out the creepy noise all by himself.

Head: All humor, no sense. At least no sense of the common variety. You may find yourself having to explain that his Karioke rendition of "Wild Thing" (performed in his underwear) may not be appropriate for your office Christmas dinner. You may then have to sit him down and calmly list the reasons why it is not a good idea for him to offer food to your boss's toupee.

A TIP... If you tell him to do something, you can be sure he will not do it. If you tell him he cannot do something, he will kill himself doing it.

Heart: A Beagle man needs "guy time." Let him go to ball games with his buddies. Let him have his regular poker night. Let him be himself and he will love you to the ends of the earth. Beagle men in good relationships are adoring, demonstrative, and forever faithful. Beagle men in bad relationships are the most miserable, irritating creatures on the planet.

Family: He's terrific with kids, shares his stuff, and unless he tries to feed his own boss's toupee, he'll probably make a pretty good living. Just keep your sense of humor and make sure you know a reliable designated driver.

Work: He'll be miserable in a Brooks Brothers suit or in any job that forces him to own one. Very bright, he's the boy wonder who shows up at the office in a Hawaiian shirt. He'd be great working in an ad agency, a dot-com startup, or in any job that mixes business with fun.

Best Match with: Funny, forgiving and extremely diplomatic women.
Bad Breed for: The anal-retentive and easily embarrassed "toe-the-line" types.

BASENJI

If I were being kind, I could describe him as eccentric. Since I'm not, I'll call him compulsive... compulsively neat, compulsively curious, compulsively fun-loving. (Warning: His sense of fun can be extremely odd.) He will demand that his bathroom and closet be kept immaculate. At the same time, you may come home to find he's turned the entire house upside-down, looking for a computer cable or his only tube of naphthamide maroon paint. Or he may be on the roof, peering at the sky through a telescope. (That's when the neighbors call to complain that the very same telescope has been seen pointing toward their bedroom window.) He's the life of the party, as long as everyone at the party does exactly what he wants them to do. This man will never accept that not everyone likes Pictionary when he pulls out the game. He refuses to believe that there might be some friends at the barbecue who do not think "nude Twister" is a good idea.

Head: The Basenji's absolute certainty that his every thought, whim, or feeling is a basic Universal Truth can be a problem. If you don't agree with him, you're a moron. If you do agree with him, you're a moron with good judgment. Once your dissenting opinion is expressed, you will be dismissed.

Heart: Nothing gets the Basenji down. You'll never find a bottle of Xanex in his medicine chest and you'll never have to try and cheer him up. He takes every rejection as if it's confirmation from God that his "most people are morons" theory is correct.

> He begins every confrontation with, "Let me tell you why you're wrong."

Family: Children need consistency. As far as the Basenji is concerned, consistency is a bore. Dinner at 5:30 every single night! What's wrong with 4:00 one day, 10:00 the next, the next day none at all? He forgot about dinner. He walked into the kitchen, then decided to build a laptop out of parts cannibalized from your kitchen appliances.

Work: The perfect job for a Basenji? Toy designer. If he's an artist, he'll create funky "Rube Goldberg" machines out of junk he's dragged home from the town dump. If he's a scientist, he'll work in a field that mainstream scientists eye with suspicion. I see him at SETI, searching deep space for signs of intelligent life. (He won't find any.)

Best Match with: Non-conformists, Basenji women.
Bad Breed for: Young Republicans, the easily exhausted.

BLACK AND TAN COONHOUND

You see an easy-going, good looking, All-American guy sitting at the kids' table at your cousin's wedding. You watch as he gently interacts with the kids, wiping tears from the face of one, playfully wrestling with another. He seems as comfortable with them as they are with him. He notices you watching, tips his cowboy hat and smiles an impishly sexy smile. He saunters toward you, a cross between Will Rogers and Adonis. Then it happens. His smile widens and he says in a quietly masculine voice, "Howdy Ma'am." You feel a bit faint. Your cheeks redden. You stammer for a moment until you are able to return a pathetic little "howdy." You've never said "howdy" in your life. Before you know it, you're spending much less time with your intellectual friends and shunning the ballet for a dance club called "Boot Scooters." Your new party list contains names like Tommy-Earl and Tammy-Sue.

Heart and Head: For a Coonhound man, heart and head are one. He's a real blue-collar man. He works really hard at really hard work and when he comes home, he want a big slab of beef, a twice-baked potato and a beer. After that, he wants you to help him pull his boots off so he can relax on the couch and watch Monday Night Football, or Wheel of Fortune, or a re-run of The Dukes of Hazard. This is who he is. The greatest sex in the world may not make up for the fact that he'll never be able to appreciate your friend Nathan's sense of humor. Or that he thinks PBS has something to do with "female problems." He won't discuss politics with you and he won't discover a cure for anything. Then again... he is awfully good looking. Or as Jane Hathaway used to say... "Oh, Jethro!"

Family: He's sweet, well meaning, hard-working, gentle-natured, great with kids and masculine without being brutish...

the perfect man for women who list "The Waltons" as their ideal TV family.

> **A Word to the Wise...** Before he punches your friend, Nathan, in a fit of jealousy, explain to him that Nathan is gay. If you don't tell him, he won't figure it out. Also, be specific when requesting dinner out at a nice restaurant. His idea of a nice restaurant is "Sizzler."

Work: He moves, he lifts, he carries, he hauls. He hammers, he drills, he sands. His garage is filled with so many tools, he no longer has room for his truck.

Best Match with: Rodeo Gals, anyone named Cheryl or Crystal.
Bad Breed for: Intellectuals, urban women, denim haters.

BLOODHOUND

He drives you crazy. He's a complete slob. He takes off with his buddies and doesn't tell you where he's going. He's gone for three days. He's totally self-involved. You're really, really mad this time. Then you slip and make eye contact. He tips his head innocently. He gazes at you with those big, sad eyes. Instantly, you melt. Your brain is certain that you're mad, but your pounding heart signals that you've made a horrible mistake. Surely this man couldn't have done anything wrong! Look at him! He's so sweet... so innocent... so hurt by your wrongful attack. You back down. Your tone changes. You give in. He tells you he loves you and you spend the next three days kicking yourself around the house. The only way to leave a Bloodhound man is to wait until he's off with his buddies on one of his weekend getaways and leave a Dear John letter. Then make sure your lawyer handles all further contact until the divorce is final. Then move to Scandinavia.

Heart: Don't think you can go to your friends with relationship problems. This man is so lovable, even your best friend from high school will hug him first when she comes for a visit.

> Bloodhound Men are often oblivious to their physical appearance. You may find yourself having to wipe mustard from his face, or reminding him to zip up. And you might have to hint that he trim his nose hair.

Head: He's completely one-tracked when he's interested in something. Early in the relationship, that something will be you. Later on, it might be tracking down the Sports Bar that has the biggest Big-Screen TV. He won't go out of his way to learn anything new, but he'll stick with a project after most have thrown in the towel.

Family: The Bloodhound is a great dad, a great friend and great fun to make up with after a fight. And you'll always be able to talk to him about your feelings. He won't change, but he will definitely listen. As your mother might say, "You could do a lot worse."

Work: Give him a mission, point him in a direction, sit back and watch. Bloodhound men will get the job done, no matter how long it takes. He's perfect for investigative work and jobs that require slow, methodical and patient pursuit. Check out Search and Rescue stations, police precincts and news organizations, if you want to meet a Bloodhound.

Best match with: Forgiving women, live-and-let-livers, suckers for sad eyes.
Bad Breed for: Man-molders, House Beautiful fans.

BORZOI
(Russian Wolfhound)

You're strolling across the plaza, arm and arm with your Borzoi man. He looks so elegant in his Armani suit. You look stunning in your Valentino gown. He kisses your hand and gazes lovingly into your eyes as you pause for a moment in front of a fountain. The moment is perfect. You try to freeze it into memory. You savor a long and passionate kiss, then pull away just far enough to utter those three magic words, "I love you…"

Before your lips can finish forming the "oooo" sound, he pulls away, pacing like a crazy person. "Why did you do that?!" he fumes, as though you had just thrown up on his Bruno Maglis. Shocked out of your moment of romantic bliss, you stand there, stunned and horrified. You don't know how to respond. He marches off to hail a cab, muttering something about you ruining everything. This is your life with a Borzoi.

Heart: Oddly, this man is kind, calm and loving 98% of the time. The problem is, you never know when to expect the 2%. It's sort of like walking through a minefield that's been swept. You're fairly confident that all is well, but what if the sweepers missed one? Just when you start to feel comfortable and begin to securely stride forth... BOOM! At the same time, he won't understand if you become angry with him or speak to him harshly.

Head: The Borzoi is smart. Weird smart. You do not want him as your partner in Trivial Pursuit unless you're playing the "Zacualpan Art History" edition.

Family: He'll only socialize with people who are like him... mainly other Sight Hound types. Adult Sight Hounds. He won't understand kids and will not enjoy their company.

Fact: This man is driven. No.. not like Bill Gates. Like the guy who continues to climb Mount Everest after the Sherpas peel off.

Work: He becomes inspired, works with god-like intensity until inspiration fades, then lies on the couch for a month, waiting for his muse to return. Yes, he knows his gallery opening is only weeks away. He can't help himself. If he's not an artist, your Borzoi is likely to be an expert in an unusual field. He may know everything there is to know about the sex lives of naked mole rats. Generally speaking, this does not pay the mortgage.

Best Match with: Supremely confident and stable women, or adrenaline junkies.
Bad Breed for: Nervous Nellies, the easily wounded.

DACHSHUND

A Dachshund man will not want to share his painful childhood experiences and will not appreciate it if you attempt to share yours. He'd rather joke off a problem than talk it through. In the middle of your heart-wrenching "how I didn't get a pony for Christmas" tale, you may look up tearfully to see a red rubber ball on the end of his nose. He's trying to lighten the mood in the middle of your catharsis. He can't handle deep, emotionally therapeutic moments. If you love him and want to stay with him, share the pony stories with your shrink and spare this dude your angst. The Dachshund is much the same with his own kind... meaning other men. He has drinking buddies, not confidants. Within his group, he's often the catalyst for misadventures. He was the guy who talked his college friends into dismantling the Dean's car and reassembling it in the library.

Head: While the Dachshund can be very focused on something he's interested in, he'll also want to know what you're up to. He'll check in with you frequently during your day. He won't mind helping you with chores, but beware! You may spend hours rearranging the things that he's rearranged after you've arranged them. He's a man with ideas, after all.

Heart: Yes, he's lovable, but be aware that Dachshund men have a bit of the con artist in them. This is a great quality if you need to find tickets to the play-off game, not so great if you suspect he has a "thing" for Sally, the new office intern. It's not so much that he lies, he's just awfully good at twisting, re-shaping, and in some cases mangling the truth. (Just a Suggestion: Go ahead and call Sally the office intern and tell her what this guy is really like. That should nip it in the bud.)

Family: The Dachsie is too much of a free spirit to be great with kids. He just doesn't want the responsibility. It's not that he doesn't like them… in fact, he's the uncle that all the kids love… it's just that he might want to go to Paris for the weekend!

Work: Though he's very bright, even intellectual, this man will do better in work that requires talent over consistency. (He's that guy who used his cell phone to call in sick from the line for the Phantom Menace opening.) If you are his co-worker, be circumspect around the Dachsie. He considers all good ideas to be his property and may swipe yours!

Best Match with: A balanced partner with a well-developed sense of humor.
Bad Breed for: Gullible gals, Gary Zukov fans, therapy addicts, privacy freaks.

FOXHOUND

Tell your friends you're going out with a Foxhound man and you'll be treated to a chorus of "Good for you's." He's as beloved by your Grandmother as he is by the kids in your neighborhood. All his ex-girlfriends still like him. His ex-wife has nothing but good things to say about him. He shares his stuff and rarely, if ever, gets into a fight. He is, in the simplest of terms, a great guy. The Foxhound is a man you'll need to keep busy. He loves a project and has trouble with the concept of doing nothing. He gets up early, and with a bit of direction from you, can finish that new deck and install the track lighting in time for the party that night. Don't expect champagne and caviar on that new deck. Your Foxhound is more the Fritos and Rolling Rock type. He'll be bored to death by conversations about stock portfolios and the latest designer fashions from Milan.

> Got a teenager of this breed? Keep an eye on his friends. If his pals are headed for trouble, he may barrel along and be in over his head before he knows it.

Head: It's not that he's slow… not exactly. Foxhound spouses often lament that they've had to learn to speak in "threes." By the third, "Honey I need some help," your Foxhound appears at the door. By the third "Honey, it's time to go," he'll amble out to the car. When he says he didn't hear you the first time, he means it.

Heart: He's a follower at heart. Though he would never dream of compromising his own integrity, he'll struggle with the idea of "ratting out" co-workers or less-than-ethical bosses. A Foxhound doesn't want to hurt people, even if they're bad people.

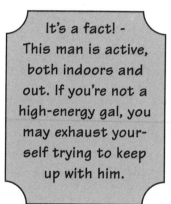

It's a fact! - This man is active, both indoors and out. If you're not a high-energy gal, you may exhaust yourself trying to keep up with him.

Family: You'll never have to beg for help with diaper changing if you're married to a Foxhound. He loves all aspects of being a dad. He'll make every school play, chauffeur them to scouts and ballgames, play endless games of Candyland and "tea party," and drift to sleep with them at some point during the fifth reading of "Goodnight Moon."

Work: The Foxhound will only be happy working as part of a group. Once he latches on to a job that interests him, he is a loyal and diligent employee. He would make an excellent assistant coach or member of a sports team. If he's in the office, he needs to specialize in one area so he can focus easily. If your Foxhound can't find his direction, he may end up wandering through life bouncing from one meaningless job to another. Help him direct his energy and hope that his boss is a Terrier.

Best Match with: Very directed women, high moral fiber gals.
Bad Breed for: Anyone of questionable moral character.

HARRIER

Excerpted from the diary of a mad Harrier housewife:

"Dear Diary... He stayed out all night gambling again. When he dragged in this morning, I'm sure I smelled the perfume of another woman. His drinking is really taking its toll on both of us. I wanted to ask what happened to the money in our savings account, but I worry it will upset him. Perhaps my undying love will help him see the error of his ways".

Snap out of it, sister! The only way a Harrier man sees the error of his ways is when you smack him in the face with a big, fat ultimatum. Until then, get used to being treated like the house-guest who stayed too long. A Harrier with a wimpy woman is a tragedy waiting to happen. It's not that he's a bad guy, he just won't rein himself in unless he truly understands that you mean business. Keep it simple. He cheats, you leave. In other words... "Get a spine!" This man really needs a no-nonsense partner, secure enough to allow him his independence, while setting firm-but-fair rules for the relationship. With the right partner, he's as playful, enthusiastic and sweet-natured as a Foxhound.

Head: All the social skills of the Foxhound, with greater intel-lectual depth. He's as comfortable making a presentation to a group of investment bankers as he is yakking with the fellows at the barbershop. While he loves being with you, the Harrier isn't dependent on you for entertainment. This makes him a natural match for a busy career woman.

Heart: Only happy when he's active, he'll need to work off his boundless energy in rigorous physical activity. If you live in a city apartment, make sure he walks whenever possible. Keep a stationary bike in the living room for rainy days. Encourage him to set up weekly ball games at the park. If you let this man sit with his energy, he'll be jumpy and anxious.

> I've seen a cooped-up Harrier man react to an elevator bell as if it were Big Ben. Trust me when I say, give this man a physical outlet!

Family: The Harrier's fun-loving temperament makes him a natural with kids and he's patient enough to put up with the noise, the demands and the constant entreaties to "play with me!" In fact, this man needs to play. You may have to step in to calm things down. He won't realize when the kids are getting tired and accidents may result.

Work: He's a self-starter, efficient and intelligent. You won't have to micromanage with a Harrier on your team. He may be a new media consultant, designing computer networks, or helping companies develop a web presence. He may be a discovery specialist with a law firm. It's essential that the Harrier understand who's in charge. If you hear him complaining that his boss is an idiot, start looking at the want ads. He won't be there long.

Best Match with: Women with backbone… determined, solid, self-confident types
Bad Breed For: Indulgent partners, pushovers, wimps

IRISH WOLFHOUND

The Irish Wolfhound man is a long, slow, lovely drink of water. He craves love and companionship and hates to be alone. With the courage and nobility of a Roundtable Knight, the Irish Wolfhound is a natural diplomat. He can bring peace into a room full of antagonists by his mere presence. But if push comes to shove, his presence is anything but mere. An Irish Wolfhound man can clear the floor just by standing and folding his arms. His protective instincts rival those of a lioness. The IW is a man that other men naturally look to for leadership. While he enjoys the companionship of most males, he has a definite preference for other Hounds. "Yappy" terrier types beware! He counts "bragging" as a character flaw and will dismiss men he feels are not hound-worthy.

Heart: The most intuitive of men, he will pick up every signal you put out. He often takes on the personality traits of those close to him. A nurturing, loving relationship will bring out the happy, affectionate side of this man. Depressing or nit-picky partners can contribute to stress-related health problems.

Head: He's a prime candidate for burnout. There are women out there who suffer from "White Knight" syndrome. They see this big, kind, capable guy and expect that he can shoulder the responsibilities and burdens for both parties. The problem with this scenario is that your Wolfhound will try to fulfill your dream and end up in the hospital or worse.

> While normally slow and calm, when he has a vision, he's as driven as Joan of Arc. Local kids need a new youth center? Just call on the nearest Irish Wolfhound Man! He'll organize community fundraising, get donations from local building suppliers, and wheedle the neighbors until they commit to working on it all weekend. He won't shy away from using his physical size to intimidate people into volunteering.

Family: The Irish Wolfhound man is extremely fond of and gentle with children. An IW dad can often be seen in the yard with six or seven kids hanging off of him. At least three or four of them belong to the neighbors. His calm demeanor and endless patience make him everyone's choice for Dad of the Year.

Work: Incredibly patient and calm, he'd make a wonderful teacher for young children. Social work and therapy are other good choices for the Irish Wolfhound man. Thanks to his kind nature and the respect he commands from others, he may be your minister, priest, or rabbi. To be an effective worker, he'll need to know the parameters of the job.

Best Match with:: Happy, glass-half-full types.
Bad Breed for: Greedies, needies, hard-to-please girls.

PHARAOH HOUND

See the man standing on the sidelines of the party, the one with regal bearing, aloof and seemingly above it all? He looks at the other guests as though he were judging horses in a show ring. You write him off as conceited… an elitist. You're about to walk away when you catch his eye. You smile. He smiles. He's cuter than you first thought. He shuffles. You move closer and notice he's... blushing? He's smiling and blushing. Conceited, elitist men don't blush. Who is this man? He's a Pharaoh Hound. Mr. Pharaoh will judge each new person on what he feels are their merits and decide if they are worthy of his attention. A welcome trait if your last few relationships have been with Sporting Dog men, who will drag just about anyone home. So, yes, he's discriminating, but given enough time he will generally warm up to any situation or environment. The First Commandment with a Pharaoh man? Never push yourself or other people on him.

Heart: When he's happy, he glows with excitement and can seem almost silly, clowning with the best of them. You won't have to baby-sit your Pharaoh, or feel guilty about taking time for yourself. A Pharaoh has an innate understanding of his partner's feelings and moods. He knows when to dive for cover or be on his best behavior. He's a fastidious man and will not be at his happiest in a filthy or chaotic home.

I've traveled all around the country asking men the question, "If you were a dog, what breed of dog would you be?" Only twice has the man replied, "I really feel more like a cat." In my opinion, both of these men were Pharoah Hounds.

Head: He's extremely intelligent and demands an Alpha partner, an equal. If he feels you are not up to the job, you will find yourself walking ten paces behind him. At the same time, if you act like his mother or his boss, he'll see every situation as a challenge and will always be thinking up ways to get the best of you. Clingy behavior will activate his natural desire to run... straight to another woman!

Family: Pharaoh men make loving, playful fathers. They are fascinated by children and are more tolerant of them than they are of most adults.

Work: The Pharaoh has an independent nature and despises repetition. He'll be at his best with his own small enterprise, or in a job that allows him to hand-pick his team. If you're his business partner, you'll have to be extremely sharp or you'll find yourself playing second fiddle. (And if you're juggling the books, or selling watered-down apple juice to third world kids, don't let this noble man find out about it. You'll be spending your next vacation in Club Fed!)

Best Match with: Equal partners, smart cookies, classy dames.
Bad Breed for: Clinging vines, big mamas, messy housekeepers.

RHODESIAN RIDGEBACK

Like the hero in a Hemingway novel, he strides across the veldt, an elephant gun on his shoulder, a strand of russet hair blowing into his ruddy, sunburnt face. A sound in the brush and he's instantly alert. Swinging into action, he spins and fires. The rogue lion, a man-eater, crashes to the ground, dead, inches from the toes of his scuffed leather boots. The man could only be a Rhodesian Ridgeback. Young boys want to be him. Women grow weak-kneed in his presence. In reality, the Ridgeback is neither a ladies man, nor a true man's man. He's so much more, well.... manly than other men that he's really in a category of his own. He's the Old Spice guy, the Marlboro man and Buck Rogers all rolled into one amazing package.

> Single moms take heed! A Ridgeback child will test your authority every chance he gets. You cannot raise this boy on your own. You will need male assistance. A priest who used to be a prizefighter would make a great mentor for this kid.

Heart: Used to being fawned over and admired, a Ridgeback takes a compliment as though accepting praise is his cross to bear in life. It's not that he's self-important. He's important, period. He won't (like the Irish Wolfhound) simply dismiss those who are not worthy of him. He'll squash them like bugs. No debating. No sparing. No compromise. They will simply be a small splatter on the bottom of his boot.

Head: In case you think that he's all muscle and not much mind, I should point out that the Ridgeback man is very intelligent, one of the smartest of the Sight Hounds. Remember... smart doesn't mean cooperative.

Family: The Ridgeback has his eye trained on the far horizon. He's not thinking about the dry cleaning or the grocery list, and he won't remember your anniversary. If you can learn to accept life on the periphery of his universe, he'll be an affectionate and trustworthy mate. Too dominant to make a great dad, his children may exhaust themselves in trying to win his love and attention.

Work: The Ridgeback is his own man and will never be happy slaving in an office cubicle. He may be a wild game warden, patrolling a preserve. He may be involved in eco-tourism, taking folks up the Amazon, or an ethnobotanist, searching the rainforest for new medicinal plants. He may well be piloting the first manned flight to Mars. The Peace Corps is a great choice for this man. He's strong enough to heave a cow out of a ditch and smart enough to learn several tribal languages on the trip over.

> Chew on this: Buck Rogers went off the air. The Old Spice Man has been replaced by brooding, tortured-looking, non-gender specific teenagers. The Marlboro Man died of lung cancer. Think about it.

Best Match with: Romance Novel Heroines.
Bad Breed for: Fragile egos, anyone who wants a real relationship.

SALUKI

You wake him up and hand him his breakfast... a ten-ounce protein and blue-green algae shake. After he's showered, you assist him in shaving all the hair off his lean and muscled body. You drive him to the speed-skating rink where you will spend your day holding a stopwatch and timing his runs. By the end of the day, he's trimmed a nanosecond off of his time. It's not enough. He's distracted and depressed. You drive him home, cook him a meal from "The Zone" diet menu and massage his aching body until you hear his breathing turn to a light snore. Then you toss back several vodka tonics while watching Jay Leno and finally pass out. This is your life with a Saluki man. The tip-off should've been the fact that he's had more short-term relationships than Hugh Hefner... the difference being that his ex-girlfriends don't speak fondly of him. Women immediately attracted by his physical beauty can find themselves repelled once they get to know the whole package.

Head: He's actually a very simple soul... a sort of "man essence." If he's a speed skater, he wakes up thinking about skating faster. If he's a businessman, he wakes up thinking about making money. The chase is everything. And this is just as true of his romantic life as it is in his work. Once he catches you, the game is over. He'll lose interest quickly.

Heart: Win his heart by playing the "impossible to get" game. You've just spent a romantic evening together, making love for the first time. Get out of his bed at three in the morning, dress and go home. Don't explain. For the next few days, don't be at home when he calls. Don't return his calls. Run into him sometime the next week, on the arm of your "old friend" Jack. Call him the next day to thank him for the flowers he sent to your office. What? He didn't send them? Wonder aloud who did. Sound like work? You betcha!

These men thrived in the 80's when self-indulgence and narcissism were all the rage. Unfortunately, for Salukis, times changed and (with the exception of professional athletes and bad "action hero" actors) society tired of egomaniacal behavior.

Family: If you ever wish to marry or think you might someday need someone to take care of you, turn and walk to the nearest exit. And if you're a gal who refuses to play games, your only course of action is to fawn, grovel, cater-to, pamper, coddle, and indulge his every whim. In this case, he'll keep you around, but treat you like "the help."

Fact: The only thing easy about this man is getting rid of him. Just bring up marriage, children, or talk about yourself for more than five minutes.

Work: He will find his "bliss" early in life and pursue it to the exclusion of all else. If he's a runner, he will run. If he's a businessman, he will eat, drink and sleep his business. He will not be derailed in his pursuit, and will be at least moderately successful at whatever he does. The crowd may cheer at the finish line, but he will never have a fan club.

Best Match with: Mirrors, reflecting pools and need-to-be needed types.
Bad Breed for: Anyone with needs of her own.

SCOTTISH DEERHOUND

Some friends introduce you to a really sweet man, a recently divorced Deerhound. You think to yourself, "He's perfect for me, but he's on the rebound. Maybe I should back off for a while, wait until he's had time to regain his equilibrium." Wrong! The next lonely woman he runs into will snap him right up. This man needs a companion. He needs a close and loving relationship. He will not wait years between marriages. So if you want him, grab him now, or some other lucky woman will. Realize that you will have to "do" for him. He can't cook his own dinner and will look at you with a blank expression if you suggest that he should. He will, however, be happy to stand behind you while you're cooking and make suggestions, or pick at the food. Some spouses of Deerhounds complain that they've pushed the car to the gas station more than once, because hubby never refills the tank. Beneath his quiet exterior, hides a restless energy that could contribute to anxiety and insomnia. Make him exercise. If you don't, he'll pace around the house behind you, getting under your skin.

Heart: He's a soft-spoken man with gentle dignity and a great big heart. He's not aggressive, but what he lacks in pushiness, he makes up for with persistence and courage.

Head: Make sure you have his full attention before making a request of him. He'll never remember to pick up the dry cleaning unless you've reminded him seven or eight times. He doesn't forget on purpose, so don't lose your temper with a Scottish Deerhound man. Easily wounded, he may hold onto the hurt for a very long time. Try using motivators to win this man's cooperation. If you want him to stop leaving clothes on the bathroom floor, try putting the hamper under a basketball hoop.

> A robber in a ski mask could walk right by him, into the house. He'd just glance distractedly at the "perp" and go back to watching the ball game.

Family: He's a devoted and faithful companion. He loves children and is a dutiful father.

Work: A Deerhound will excel in a job that can be broken into component parts, so that he can learn each part thoroughly before putting the parts together. Once he's decided what he wants to do in life, he'll be very good at that one thing and not much interested in anything else. (He declared his college major in second grade.) He will not have a hobby or a second career. As a result, the retirement years may be difficult for a

Deerhound. It's not that the old dog couldn't learn a few new tricks, he just really doesn't want to.

Best Match with: Women who don't mind "doing for."
Bad Breed for: Disorganized, pampered, or childish women.

WHIPPET

Before you dismiss that cute Whippet guy, because you fear that he may snap like a twig during sex, there's something you should know about Whippets. They're much tougher than they appear to be. Not Jesse Ventura tough, more like Evel Knievel. Resilient. Okay... romantically speaking, he probably won't satisfy a woman with "Conan the Barbarian" fantasies, but let's not underestimate stamina. Whippet men are anything but frail. What he may lack in physical size and brute strength, he more than makes up for in willpower and enthusiasm. These men are frequently misjudged on the basis of their appearance. Some take Whippets to be cold and aloof, due to their aristocratic bearing, when in fact, they are quite loving and demonstrative. Don't confuse his boundless enthusiasm with nervousness either. Energetic doesn't always mean neurotic. You'll have to remind him to eat, and to eat well. He's an eat-on-the-run type and a steady diet of fast food will not be good for him.

Heart: He won't boss you, you won't have to pick up after him and you'll never have to have that "you embarrassed me tonight" talk. This guy can harness his energy in appropriate ways. When you need quiet, he's quiet. When you need action, he's more than ready to oblige. He could possibly put a stop to those silly Conan fantasies forever.

Head: He's smart enough to make a good living, but you'll never lose him to his job. He doesn't have the cutthroat mentality of a high powered executive. His boss will love him because he's focused and gets things done. His co-workers will love him because he'll never be a threat to them. He's not a ladder climber or a head-stepper.

Family: No suspicious "I'm working late" phone calls from your Whippet man. He cherishes his time at home with you and is supremely loyal once committed. The only complaint your kids may have is that they will have to seek out a neighborhood "Working Dog" dad if they want to rough-house. Whippet men don't gravitate toward sports that require a great deal of physical contact. Terrific soccer dad. Not a great football dad.

Work: He's not likely to be a neurosurgeon or a high-priced corporate lawyer, but when he's working, he's totally focused. Like other Sight Hound men, he is adept at seeing things others cannot. Your Whippet may have a job that keeps him on the go, dashing around the city, flagging cabs, always on his way to a meeting.

Best Match with: Caretakers, easy-goers.
Bad Breed for: Conan fanatics, Ivana Trump wannabes.

Working Dogs at Work and Play

WORKING DOG MEN

He won't even consider putting an alarm system in the house! Why should he? He's there. And this man has the bite to back up his bark. If he tells you he's working late at the office? He means it! He'll insist on doing the driving. If you tell him that you like to open doors for yourself, he will never understand. Why should you risk breaking your pretty pink nails when he can lift that heavy box? If you've ever caught yourself thinking, "Whatever happened to all the real men?"... Or if you're the kind of woman who dreams of being swept off your feet by that knight on a white horse, there could be a Working Dog in your future.

Like his canine counterparts, who were bred to guard herds, patrol grounds, and perform rescues, the Working Dog Man is territorial. He may or may not be wildly successful, but whether his collar is white or blue, he judges himself by his ability to support and protect his family. He may be a doctor, or a hospital orderly... a police commissioner, or a night watchman... on the board of the Sierra Club, or a forest ranger, patrolling a national park. When you find him in business, he the guy who looks out for those working under him. Television's Cliff Huxtable, of the Cosby Show, was a Working Dog man, but so was Roseanne's Dan Conner.

On the dark side of the Working Dog force, we find dictators, control freaks, and worrywarts. These men are too protective, too territorial, too dominant, and just too plain big for their britches. If you let him, the negative Working Dog Man will be only too happy to run your life for you. Either lay down the law to him, or sit back and watch as your home becomes a prison.

Porch Dogs

A small sub-set of the Working Dog group, the Hauling Dogs are less territorial and possessive than their fellows. For some women, this makes them easier to live with than other Working Dog Men. Note that I said "for some women." Hauling Dog Men are also more extroverted and much more likely to chase a passing skirt.

AKITA

You say you're tired of whiney, clingy mama's boys? Been searching for a strong, silent type? You might want to take a look at Mr. Akita. If you choose him, you'll never have to hear yourself use that tired old line, "I need more space." Just don't be fooled by his cool confidence. Phone calls from old boyfriends will not sit well with this man. Still, you've got to be an independent woman to be with an Akita. He'll tell you to go to the party and let him stay home, so learn to RSVP for one. He's not a cuddler. He will not fawn over you. He will, however, throw himself in front of a train for you, if he sees that train as a danger to his gal. Let us repeat, this is not a man for wimps. He needs a strong woman, but is better with an Earth Mother than with a pushy broad. You'll feel very secure with him.

Head: In a word? Hard. Most of your fights will end with, "Let's just agree to disagree," because he'll never give in.

Heart: The Akita man is loyal to a fault. Though he doesn't wear his heart on his sleeve, he gives that heart completely. If he is widowed, he may never marry again.

Family: He'll be a good dad to his kids, but he won't volunteer to lead the scout den, as he doesn't care that much for other people's kids. And he won't be afraid to step in with discipline, if he thinks his kids are "running with the wrong crowd."

Work: The Akita man would make a great secret service agent... having the strength to run down and tackle a suspect, ready to take a bullet for his president, able to blend in quietly at diplomatic functions. He has great dignity. If he finds a cause close to his heart, he'll work for it tirelessly. If he likes you enough to work for you, he'll be true blue. You'll never have to worry about him stealing your files, when he leaves you for another firm. Possible negatives? He's a bit of a loner. He'll have trouble cooperating with other members of a team. The Akita is not a creative type. If you're looking for cutting edge or high concept, look elsewhere.

Best Match with: Strong, secure, Earth Mother types.
Bad Breed for: Wimps, or overly aggressive women.

ALASKAN MALAMUTE

Who's that guy on the beach saying, "Feel my muscle," as he flexes for bystanders? You can be pretty sure he's our Malamute. It's hard to resist this cheerful, enthusiastic, magnanimous man. Before you get too enthralled though, make sure you check your own insecurities at the door. Yes, he's a Worker, but he's also one of the Hauling breeds, and is more likely to stray. You must set boundaries early in the relationship. Don't wait until he's crossed the line to let him know that there is one. Bad habits are hard to break for the Malamute. And, you'll have to keep reminding him of what your boundaries are. He gets caught up in the moment and forgets. He'll rummage through your drawers, when looking for his wallet, leaving the contents scattered across the bed. The idea that he might be violating your privacy would never occur to him. You'll have to tell him. And, you'll have to repeat yourself. More than once.

Heart: All that attracts you to this man attracts everyone else to him. If your neighbor is a Victoria's Secret model, you may want to think about moving. If your neighbor is the mousy town librarian, you may want to think about moving. Sorry, but women love a Malamute and he loves them.

Head: Before you move in with a Malamute, make sure you have plenty of projects lined up to keep him busy. He enjoys physical labor and, on a whim, might just decide to knock out a wall and expand your kitchen. This all seems great until you realize that he knows nothing about wiring and can't tell sheet rock from shingle.

Family: There are some fathers who are fine with older kids, but have no idea what to do with an infant, and our Malamute is one of these. He's also not great with shy, nervous children. He'll want his kids to play ball and go rock climbing with him. He's a great dad for a junior jock, not so great for a budding Picasso.

Work: You'll find him in jobs that put him around people. He'd make a great salesman. He'd excel in public relations work. He won't last long in a job where he's forced to take orders. He makes money, but is not good at managing it. If he owns a restaurant, he'll want to work the bar, buying far too many drinks for friends. His wife will have to make sure the IRA's are funded. For those who work with him, he's the front man, you'll have to take care of the details.

Best Match with: Patient, sensible women.
Bad Breed for: Jealous or insecure women

BERNESE MOUNTAIN DOG

If your idea of bliss is marriage, a passel of kids, and a house with the white picket fence, look no further than the Bernese Mountain Dog. A "Bernie" lives for family vacations, summer barbecues, and PTA meetings. Cooperative and adaptable, he's up for anything and enjoys all sorts of activities. Ask him if he wants to go with you to a ballgame, he'll say, "Sure!" Ask him if he wants to go with you to the opera, he'll say, "Sure!" As long as it's with you, he'll go. But, he's just as happy to stay at home in front of the TV, with the kids piled on top of him. And where can you find this lovely man? Check with your local Big Brother organization for a list of volunteers. Look for family-owned businesses with names like, "Jones and Son's." Don't waste your time searching for him at the local pick-up bar. He's not that kind of guy. Your married girlfriends will want to set you up with him, so don't turn down that blind date. He may turn out to be a Bernie!

Head and Heart: There is a minor downside to this lovable guy. He's not great for women who "vant to be alone." Think a weekend spa retreat with the girls sounds like fun? Not if you're married to a Bernese Man. It's not that he won't let you go, it's just that he'll call every ten minutes to ask where something is, or when you're coming home. How could you ever go without him?

> My friend, Maggie, has a Bernese Mountain Dog husband and a Bernese Mountain Dog of the four-footed variety. She says they both like to lie in front of the television and have their tummies rubbed.

Family: As a parent, he's impossible to compete with. Make sure you can handle the fact that your kids will sprint past you to greet him at the door with a loud and enthusiastic, Daddy!

Work: Owing to his adaptability, he's able to work in many occupations. You're more likely to find a Bernie in a small business than a large corporation, as he's more comfortable when his co-workers feel like family. He might be the owner of the local mom and pop market. He may be self-employed and working out of his home. He will definitely not be a corporate lawyer or a traveling salesman.

Best Match with: A wide variety of women.
Bad Breed for: Workaholics, those who travel a lot.

BOXER

Buy a pair of good cross-trainers and pop in your workout tape, you're in for a ride! Forget about that leisurely morning in bed, reading the Sunday Times. Your Boxer guy is a fitness fanatic. His idea of a great honeymoon is hiking the Andes, or mountain biking cross-country. Even if his sport of choice isn't something you can participate in, he'll expect you to be there watching. Watching HIM, that is. Don't think you can read a book during the third quarter because you will be quizzed about his every magnificent move later that evening. But who can get mad at this guy? A combination of chiseled good looks and tail-wagging enthusiasm, your Boxer guy isn't conceited, he's just really pleased with himself.

> So you know! You can find your Boxer man at the gym, at the High School track, or playing Frisbee in the park. The quickest way to his heart? Join the game!

Head: As friendly and outgoing as he may seem at home, the Boxer man isn't always Mr. Gregarious at parties. You may find yourself with a shadow at your next wedding reception, office dinner, or Bar Mitzvah. It's not that he'll clam up when you're out, he just wants you to break the ice for him with strangers... then stick around and listen to him talk.

Heart: So you're at that party and he's stuck to you like glue? You can sneak away from him for a minute, just make sure you don't look too enthralled with your ex-boyfriend's amusing story. He will be jealous. Not "punch the guy in the nose" jealous... more like "sad and distant and you don't know why" jealous. He needs your attention to feel good about himself.

Family: The Boxer man is a great choice if you want to have kids. And it may be that the only break you get in this relationship, is when he runs outside to play with them. Enjoy the freedom while it lasts. Come retirement, he's the guy who wants to sell the house, buy the RV and spend his golden years touring the world with you.

Work: Your Boxer man is a hard worker. He'll bring home a decent paycheck. But don't expect a CEO's salary, as he likes to play as well. You'll find him in service fields. He may be a fire fighter, a personal trainer, or a track and field coach. The Boxer is an energetic employee, his cheerful presence helping to build morale among his fellows. He's the guy who'll organize the company baseball team.

Best Match with: High energy women, runners.
Bad Breed for: Couch potatoes, loners.

BULLMASTIFF

The Bullmastiff man is a practical sort. If you want him to do something, give him a good reason and he'll do it. If you can't come up with a good reason, you may as well move on to the next request. He's not going to budge. Okay, he might budge a little, if you give him a back rub and tell him how wonderful he is. Maybe. Just don't tug too hard on his leash, unless you want him to tug back. You definitely won't have to worry about burglars with a Bullmastiff man in the house. His home is his castle and he doesn't cotton to outsiders who would up and take what is his. Once he's in for the night, he's in until morning. Look for him in the E-Z-Boy, or the over-sized hammock. So, he's not the neatest guy in the world, but neither is he a lazy slob. Learn to live with a little mess, or learn to like housework, is our advice. He's calm, quiet, and easy to live with under normal circumstances, but will never allow anyone to threaten his family. Once his anger is aroused, he will never back down.

Heart: Don't let this tower of strength fool you. He needs, needs, needs your love and attention. Basically a "one-woman man," a Bullmastiff will be miserable married to a social butterfly. He's no extrovert and will be jealous if you flirt with other guys. (It would be a rare man who would dare flirt with you in front of a Mastiff husband!)

Head: The man's no dummy. A Mastiff learns quickly and has buckets of common sense. He'll probably never be an astrophysicist, but he's the kind of guy who could quietly sock away a million dollars, while working at an ordinary job.

Family: Fiercely loyal to his family, he makes a terrific dad, loves kids, and will really be in his element once a child reaches that "wrestle on the floor" age. Look in the backyard of a Bullmastiff man and you'll find the elaborate tree house and swing set he's built for his lucky kids.

92

Work: He's a hard-working, no nonsense, nose to the grindstone kind of guy. The Bullmastiff man may be a football lineman (never the quarterback or receiver), a bouncer in a nightclub, or a construction foreman. Look for him doing manly work, among other manly men. He'll be the guy that the other guys look to as leader. And, he looks really sexy in a tool belt.

Best Match with: Frugal, sensible women, full-time moms.
Bad Breed for: Social climbers, party girls, spendthrifts, pushovers.

DOBERMAN PINSCHER

Your Dober-Man's got a line on a job that's perfect for him and you feel great. But, he has a bout of insecurity on the very day of the job interview, blows the job, stops for a drink on the way home, and manages to provoke a bar fight. Boy, are you upset! You bail him out, take him home, and he balls up on the couch for hours, all apologies and neurotic soul searching. How could you ever have been mad? You soften up and your attempts to comfort him turn into a night of wild lovemaking. Life is grand! Then, you wake up to find him arguing heatedly with your neighbor over exactly where the property line lies and the neighbor threatens a lawsuit. So, on his way to buy hot wire to keep the neighbor out of his yard, he runs into an old pal who offers him the perfect job... for twice the money the other job paid! Why were you ever worried? He always comes through, doesn't he?

Head and Heart: "I'm searching for a really good-looking, but tortured man. One who will protect me and cuddle with me. A guy who's confident, yet insecure… macho, and at the same time, sensitive… an athlete, with a complex mind… fearless, yet respectful of my needs… passionate, but with restraint. Maybe a Navy Seal who cries at Hallmark commercials?" You, my dear, are looking for a Dober-Man, for he is all these things and more. The problem is, you'll never know when you're going to get what!

A MUST-DO!
Meet his family. If they seem stable, give him a chance. If they seem crazy… run like the wind!

Family: Not stable enough to make a good dad, and thrown into confusion by the constant activity of children, he may do fine as half of a couple… especially if your half is calm, patient, and down to earth. If you can handle him, he'll adore you.

Work: If your boss is a Doberman, prepare yourself for conflicting orders and memos that render the work you just finished unnecessary. If he's your employee, stock up on Maalox. On the other hand, he might be the guy who invents the "pet rock" and becomes suddenly wealthy… or makes you wealthy. You never know with a Doberman.

Best Match with: Women who are easily bored.
Bad Breed for: Those with high blood pressure, recovering addicts.

GIANT SCHNAUZER

So, you think his macho, drill sergeant personality is cute. His ducks are sooooo in a row! He's never wishy-washy! He establishes order in the midst of chaos! He's so manly! Besides, you can change him, right? Wrong! The Giant Schnauzer man was, is, and always will be exactly what he is. He won't just put order in your life; he will run your life. You'll be on his schedule. You'll watch what he wants to watch, eat what he wants to eat, do what he wants to do. The word compromise is not in this man's vocabulary. Maybe if you're a woman whose life is completely out of control, your house is a mess, your finances are in shambles, you can't pick out your own clothes, your VCR is blinking, your engine block has cracked because you never check your car's oil, and you're still convinced you can give yourself a good home perm, you should take a look. Otherwise... Be afraid, be very afraid!

Heart: Yes, he's certainly bold and on a good day can be playful and fun loving. But if you tend to be a doormat, by pairing up with a Giant Schnauzer, you'll be assuring your status as the World's Greatest Doormat. Statues will be erected in your likeness. Sally Jesse Raphael and Jenny Jones will invite you to appear as a guest on their shows.

Head: Hardheaded hardly describes him. If you have any opinions, you will end up devoting your life to fighting with him. You'll go from pleading, to demanding, to screaming, to hurling large objects.

Family: Like the dad in "Cheaper by the Dozen," he'll run his home like an assembly line, requiring morning dress inspections, putting his kids through random drug tests, and checking everyone's bed-making skills by bouncing quarters off the top-sheet.

Work: Working for him is no picnic. There is no employee day care or bring-your-kid-to-work day. He does not have an open door policy. If you've got a problem, take it to your bartender. There is no suggestion box. It's even worse to have him working under you, as he ignores your requests and is constantly challenging your authority.

Warning! The most extreme GS man could move his family to a compound in Montana, to spend his days patrolling the perimeter with an assault rifle and praying for intruders.

Best Match with: Lost causes, survivalists.
Bad Breed for: Women with their own ideas.

GREAT DANE

A big, sweet, even-tempered, very predictable guy, a Dane is well-meaning, good-hearted, friendly and social. Okay, he's not the quickest train on the track, more like the little engine that could. He'll get there, it's just that it may take him a bit more time. Of course, after many relationships with brainy, neurotic men, the Great Dane man can be refreshing. And, boy oh boy! Does he ever look impressive! Sad sacks and moody gals should steer clear of the Dane man. He needs a cheerful mate to feel cheerful himself. He won't trust a woman he feels is yanking his leash and he won't know how to pull you out of the depths of despair. He'll try, of course, but his suggestions will border on the ridiculous and will only serve to depress you more.

Heart and Head: Life has no shades of gray for a Dane. He's not very adaptable and is unlikely to see change as good. This means that he's often unprepared when change knocks on his door. If he loses his job, and can't find another in his area of expertise, it will be painful for him to have to learn a new trade. Should he lose his spouse, the many adjustments he'll have to make in his everyday life will seem overwhelming. This is not to say that the Dane's not up for a good adventure, he just needs to know that the adventure will be one that he understands. In other words a move from a ranch in New Mexico to a farm in Wisconsin would sound fine to him. Just don't try to move him from his ranch to an apartment in Boston or Chicago. If you take him out of his element he will feel insecure and miserable.

Family: A loving husband and father, neither jealous nor possessive. He's kind, affectionate, emotionally stable. He tends to be permissive with his kids, so it's not likely they will be rebels. If they are? He'll be hurt. He won't understand.

Work: He goes to work every day. He supports his family. He buys savings bonds for the kids. But, he'll never make VP and he'll never start his own business. You'll find him on the assembly line. He may be a plumber or carpenter. He's the much talked about, and recently endangered, skilled laborer. Many great Great Dane men have been put out of work, when companies downsize or move overseas. And if his job becomes obsolete, it's hard for him to shift gears, learn a whole set of new tricks. If you are his boss, know that if mistakes happen, they are never intentional. A Dane is dedicated and reliable, and is often the guy who gets promoted past his ability to cope with the job. Many Great Danes, however, will refuse the promotion, citing the demands of family as the reason. He likes the simpler path and is more concerned with being content than being promoted.

Best Match with: Cheerful, "white picket fence" types.
Bad Breed for: Intellectuals, eccentrics, snobs, therapy addicts.

GREAT PYRENEES

You're right in the middle of a great episode of "ER," your favorite show, when suddenly, an imposing figure enters the room. He makes a beeline for the remote, flips to an episode of "Walker, Texas Ranger," and plops down in his favorite chair. It's as if you're not even there. "I was watching something," you say, as he stares at Chuck Norris, who is kick-boxing someone's teeth in on the set. You tell him again, more emphatically this time. He slowly turns in your general direction and mutters something under his breath. He didn't see you… or something along those lines. You notice as he turns that he is eating a large ice-cream sundae. Don't bother asking if he made you one. He didn't. In fact, there's no ice-cream left. He's eaten it all. It didn't occur to him that you might want some. This is your world now. You married a Great Pyrenees. It seemed like a good idea a few years ago, when you first met him. He was so big and strong, so sure of himself, so confident, so virile. Sure, there were warning signs. Like the time he punched out the UPS guy, because he thought you were having an affair. Then, there was that time he forgot to pick you up at the airport, because his game went into overtime. And why did you stay with him after he took off on that ski weekend with his buddies, without telling you where he was going, or when he would be back. Hey! Stop whining! You married the guy. This is who he is. He doesn't do it to upset you. He really does love you. He's been telling you all along that he is totally self-involved. So, what do you do when you find yourself attracted to a Great Pyrenees man? Velcro the remote to your garter belt, hide the ice-cream, and learn a few good wrestling holds. Or... you can find yourself a different man.

Head: This is not a "fuzzy logic" kind of guy. He lives in a world of black and white, YES and NO, my way or the highway.

Heart: Look on the bright side. He's not going to cheat on you.

Family: He'll expect a lot of his kids, but he'd go to the ends of the earth to help them. You might want to pray for boys, though. While a Newfoundland dad can be tough on a dating-age daughter, a Great Pyrenees dad won't want his daughter to date at all. It will be your job to sneak her out of the house, so that she can meet up with her boyfriend.

Work: The Great Pyrenees is a natural boss, so don't expect him to be just another member of your team. If he's in the military, he's an officer. If he's on the loading dock, he's the foreman. He's the consultant who is called into a failing company to whip things into shape. Or he's the CEO who buys that failing company, trims the fat, fires the incompetent, and squeezes a huge profit from it.

Best Match with: Thick-skinned, ballsy gals.
Bad Breed for: Passive-aggressive women, anxious, easily hurt women.

KOMONDOR

> TAKE HEED! If you're the kind of woman who writes love letters to imprisoned serial killers, please, read on. If not, you may move directly to the next dog.

What can I say about the Komondor man? Yes, he is attractive in a "Wild Bunch" sort of way. He's also quite energetic. Not in that "jogs ten miles a day" way, more like the "five carjackings an hour" way. Try combining enormous physical size, with a propensity for aggressive behavior, and a low IQ, and you've got a pretty good idea what you're in for. This dude is trouble with a capital T. Are you getting the message? Don't go out with a Komondor! He's not the guy your mother warned you about, he's the guy the prison warden warned you about. Don't marry him. Don't have kids with him. Don't introduce your friends to him. Let me remind you, once again... there are no bad breeds of dogs, just bad breeds of men. This is one of them. If you still want to find him, try looking in maximum-security prisons and terrorist camps.

Head: He can figure out how to do something ... if he wants to. Unfortunately, outside of cracking a safe or cracking a head, there's not much "want to" in this guy.

Heart: Okay, okay... he might crack a funny joke after a few beers and make you laugh for a minute. Just don't laugh too loud or too long at his joke. He might get irritated and punch you. On the other hand, you'll feel safe from intruders when he's in the house. Of course, you may find yourself longing for an intruder to pop in, when he's in a bad mood.

Family: For the love of Pete... don't do it.

Work: He may be a drug dealer, or an enforcer for the mob. He may be the neck-snapping instructor at one of those Soldier of Fortune mercenary training schools. Too dumb to make a good boss, too mean to employ for grunt work, you shouldn't hire this guy, any more than you should marry him.

Best Match with - Suicides-in-training.
Bad Breed for - Anyone else with a pulse.

NEWFOUNDLAND

The worst thing you can say about him is that he's messy. He falls asleep on the sofa and snores and drools. He leaves his clothes on the floor. He doesn't put his dishes in the sink. He leaves the top off the toothpaste. He leaves lots of hair in the bathtub. Don't marry this guy if you're a compulsive neatnik, are easily annoyed, or have a martyr complex. Or do marry him and hire a maid. He makes enough money for you to hire a maid. Remember, he's not being messy to annoy you. He's just a big, sweet, lovable slob.

Head and Heart: What a marshmallow! He doesn't get mad at you. He doesn't understand when you get mad at him. Because he loves you so much, the Newfoundland man can be an overzealous protector. He won't worry about prowlers breaking into your house, and he's too gregarious to move the family to a compound, but he will worry about the dangers lurking in the outside world. If he sees you walking out the door, on the way to go shopping, he'll say, "Why don't I drive you? I don't like that covered parking lot at the mall. They don't have enough overhead lighting."

Family: The kids won't be allowed to swim at the beach unless he's right beside them, holding their hands and re-tying their life vests. The daughter of a Newfoundland dad won't have an unescorted date until she's twenty and, even then, he'll follow her in his car. It's not that he doesn't trust her... it's not even that he doesn't trust her date... it's just that "you never know what might happen out there."

FYI ... Your girl children will be "Daddy Crazy" until they hit their teens, at which point they will turn to you for help in sneaking out to meet their boyfriends.

Work: People will stand in line to hire this guy. You may find him in jobs that have to do with safety... building inspector, wilderness adventure guide, Child Protective Services. In business, he's the guy with the horribly messy desk that will nevertheless be a real stickler when it comes to safety in the workplace. If he's a contractor, he'll never cut corners just to save money. As he's so likable, he'll be good at managing others and his concern for his people will extend into their lives outside of the job.

Best Match with: Loving, patient live-and-let-livers.
Bad Breed for: Prissy Peggys, irritable or extremely independent women.

NORWEGIAN ELKHOUND

Forget the "hound" in Elkhound. This guy is not hound-like in any way. He's 100% pure Hauling Dog Man. Think "Emotional Viking"... a tough guy who wears his heart on his sleeve. You will never have to guess what the Elkhound man is feeling. He won't just say he's bored, he'll flop around the house, moaning and bouncing things off the wall. When he's frustrated, he may put his fist through the wall. Things going well? He's not just happy. He's ecstatic! Going badly? He won't cry, he'll wail. This man lives life to the fullest. He pops the stamp off the edge of every envelope and has a great time doing it. Though naturally extroverted, there are times he wants to be social and times that he doesn't... times he's extremely loving and times he really wants to be alone.

Head: It's not because he's erratic or unreliable. He's actually quite steady. It's just that, according to him, there's a time and place for everything. He lives in the moment and each moment has its own flavor. (If the flavor of the moment is an attractive woman, it may require a swift kick from you to bring him to his senses.)

Heart: Be prepared to lay down the law, then deal with the fact that he will break it. If you tell him dinner will start at 7:00, he'll show up at 7:10. Explain that the party is formal, he'll rent the tux, but wear his old tennis shoes with it. Don't treat this man like a retriever. The first time you ask him to run to the store, he may do it. The second time, he'll tell you to go yourself. The third time, he'll tell you to go to hell.

Family: The Elkhound can be too self-serving for some children. There will be times he doesn't want to be around kids. Children tend to have their own agendas and could care less if he's in one of his "moods". Small or sensitive children will be hurt when he's not interested in their book report or forgets to fawn over their drawing. He'll be better with older, tougher kids who are past the age where they care so intensely about what their parents think.

Work: He doesn't work for the thrill of it. If he's a lawyer, you won't find him in the public defenders office, or working for the ACLU. He expects to be paid well for his work, so he won't file that civil suit for three wronged clients. When it comes to class action, fourteen is his magic number. Any less and he won't make his money. But, once he's taken the case, he'll stick in to the bitter end, doing his best for his clients, and knocking down anyone who gets in his way. Thanks to his high intelligence, many fields are open to the Elkhound. And because he's an "alpha," he's likely to succeed. You won't find him in fields that require close cooperation with others.

Best Match with: Outdoorsy, social partners and firm-but-fair types.
Bad Breed for: Uptight, fragile, or submissive women.

Note: Some authorities put the Elkhound in the Hound group, thanks to a mistranslation of his Norwegian name. For our purposes, this breed does not belong with the hounds, as he does not resemble a hound in any way. I have chosen to place him in the Working Dog group, along with the other Hauling Dogs, to whom he is actually related.

ROTTWEILER

The first thing you need to do when you find yourself attracted to a Rottweiler is... MEET HIS MOTHER! In fact, meet his whole family. If no immediate family members are in jail or in hiding, you can consider a date with him. If there's no history of mental illness in his family, you can date him regularly. Date him for a loooooong time. Put him to the test. See how he reacts in every imaginable situation before you commit. Show up late for dinner. Wear clothes you know he doesn't like. Have your mother drop by frequently. Invite your neighbor's kids to use your yard for ballgames. See how he reacts when you tell him that you've asked your best friend Todd to be your maid of honor. Are you getting the message? Know your Rottweiler!

Head: He will think hard before he commits, but once he commits, he considers the relationship a done deal. To his mind, you belong to him. True, no one will dare break into your house, but what happens when you want to break out of your house? Good luck! On the other hand... he is a hunk. If the main thing you want from a relationship is to feel protected, the Rottweiler may be the guy for you.

Heart: On the other hand, he probably won't cheat on you (and he's not the kind of man you'd want to be caught cheating on). The Rottweiller will bring home a check, he just won't bring you flowers. If you are a bottomless pit of nurture, patience, and understanding, with no real needs of your own, this could be a match made in heaven.

Family: He'll support his kids, but they can forget about cuddling up on daddy's lap. Kid cuddling will be your job. When he comes home, he wants to see them bathed and lined up in their pajamas, then it's off to bed, lights out, no mess, no problems. When he says, "Don't make me come in there!" he really means it. He won't want the kids to mess with his things... his stereo, his car, anything in his tool chest, anything electronic, anything he paid good money for, anything at all.

Work: He may be a career military man, a bounty hunter, a prison guard, or a beat cop in a big city. But, as the German Shepherd is our good cop, the Rottweiler is often the bad cop, as his emotions can run away with him.

Best Match with: Female bodhisatvas and goddesses of self-denial.
Bad Breed for: Women who have opinions or women who have gun permits.

SAINT BERNARD

Finally! A man you'll never have to remind to take out the garbage! Once he understands what his chores are, a Saint Bernard is only too happy to oblige. It's hard not to love this big, sweet, hard-working and lovable lug. What you see is what you get with Mr. Saint Bernard. No big surprises, no mid-life crises and, best of all, he's happy to take care of the kids! There's also no worry about burglars with this guy in the house. His mere presence is more of a burglar deterrent than any rifle. You can tell him about your ex-boyfriends, flirt with the bag boy at the grocery, ask for a male masseur at the spa, join the Brad Pitt fan club. It won't bother him! He's not the jealous type! And get this... he'll let you wear his shirts, drive his new car, borrow his tools and open a joint checking account with him, because he's not possessive either! Be still my beating heart!

Head: He's willing to do anything for you as long as you ask in the right way. Domineering women might want to steer clear of him. So should weak, passive types. If you're strong enough to put him in his place once in awhile, and smart enough to know how to get around him, he's a dream hubby. But never give him an ultimatum! He'll shut right down.

Heart: There may be one tiny little problem with a St. Bernard man. Sometimes he's so busy taking care of people and organizing neighborhood stick ball games, he doesn't notice that you need him. It never occurs to him that it might be inconvenient to have his buddy's entire family stay with you while they're remodeling their house.

Family: With kids, he's a natural. Many moms worry when the kids are out with dad, but not the wife of a Saint Bernard Man. He's Mr. Mom in a big, burly package.

Work: This man is a true hero and a big proponent of teamwork. You may see him on CNN, organizing an airlift of food to starving refugees. If he's a Clergyman, he's sure to be an activist, helping the homeless or working with prison inmates. At work he's the foreman or the manager of his group. Never jealous of his co-workers, he believes that if they look good, he looks good. He needs physical work, so if he has a desk job, make sure he has projects on the weekends.

Best Match with: Community-minded women, almost everybody.
Bad Breed for: Sadists or Masochists.

SAMOYED

Everybody knows a Samoyed man. Everybody's dated a Sammy. He's in every black book and on every party list. If he's not on the list, he's at the party anyway. Don't worry, you won't have to throw him out, you'll be too busy being entertained by him. He makes you feel good. He makes you laugh. He makes you feel special. You hear everyone saying, "I love that guy!" You hear yourself saying, "I love that guy!" But, if you're the jealous type, beware! Like other men in the Hauling Dog subgroup, he has a tendency to roam. His greatest asset is his greatest flaw. He just loves women! He's no womanizing cad, he just loses himself in the moment.

Head: If you call him on his bad behavior, he'll try to get around you with those big, blue eyes and that winning smile. Most of the time, he'll succeed. But the situation isn't hopeless. If he's sure that you're committed, he'll be much more likely to stay near home.

Heart: You could worry that with a heart this big, there may be room in there for more than just you. He really can't help that women find him attractive. Try steering him clear of situations that might be tempting for him. Freedom with boundaries is the best tactic.

Family: The Sammy loves kids. Makes sense. He's just a big kid himself... the dad every kid in the neighborhood thinks is cool. But he may not always be watching while he's having fun with the kids. Many a wild romp with a Sammy dad has ended in the emergency room. Like a kid, the Sammy is messy, leaving his junk all over the house. Who has time to clean, when there's all this life to be lived?

Work: He's a "follow your bliss" man. If he finds his job boring, he won't be able to stand it, and will be an unreliable employee. Sam's have no patience with busy work. If it's not essential, why waste his time? He'll be best in a job that makes use of his winning personality and charm... the guy that closes the deal, never the accountant in the back room. He might be a restaurant manager. He'd be great as a fundraiser for a cause he truly cares about. With all that charisma, he could be an actor, but you'd probably find him acting in the soaps, rather than in something risky and avant garde.

Best Match with: The generous, the forgiving, the free-spirited.
Bad Breed for: Jealous Nellies, Grinches, those who hate to share.

SIBERIAN HUSKY

He's the center of the party... that incredibly magnetic and energetic man, surrounded by a group of enthralled admirers? You move closer, drawn in by his animated facial expressions, the joy that radiates from his face as he reenacts his latest freestyle skiing adventure. Who is this man? He's so dynamic! So adventurous! So daring and free-spirited! Then he sees you. Your heart pounds! He smiles at you. Your knees weaken! He approaches. You feel faint! "Hi there," he says with a boyish grin, "I'm a Siberian Husky. Who are you?" Birds begin chirping, romantic music swells... WAIT! Rewind that tape. There are a few things you should know before you book the wedding chapel. First of all, he smiles at all the girls that way.

Head: He's very smart. I said smart... not obedient. Don't try to boss him. It won't make him mad. It'll make him leave. His very restless mind needs constant stimulation. He may demand that you pick up and move on a moment's notice. He will expect you to ski off the mountain with him. If he gets bored for a minute, he's out of there. Once he decides to go, you cannot stop him.

Heart: He's a real people person, a "more the merrier" kinda guy, which is only a problem because he's never picky about who he invites into the house. Could be a best-selling novelist, could be someone on the FBI's ten most wanted list.

Family: Don't get too discouraged. He's totally great with kids. Just make sure they have helmets and knee pads.

WARNING! The negative Husky man can be a real hustler, financing get-rich schemes with other people's money. He can talk a woman out of her savings in a minute, flat!

Work: He'll always work, but every time he threatens to make money in a given career, he changes jobs. Whatever you do, don't expect a Siberian Husky man to settle down. He can't do it. That's why a lot of these men choose careers as truck drivers, or pilots for small airlines. He might like racecar driving. Lots of speed, lots of attention.

Best Match with: Brave souls who can go with the flow.
Bad Breed for: Those frightened of change.

STANDARD SCHNAUZER

So, you just broke up with your Giant Schnauzer boyfriend because you couldn't handle his macho attitude. All those fights, all those nights you left at three AM because he was trying to control your life. You can't believe you stayed with him so long! But, he was so smart, so organized, so in control, so... impossibly anal! Before you run back for more heartbreak, you might want to take a good look at a Standard Schnauzer. He's Giant Schnauzer Lite... all the intelligence and drive of his brother, with fewer "control freak" tendencies. No need to worry about finances, either. A Schnauzer Man will be an excellent provider. There will be cash in the checking account and in the retirement fund. As long as you don't mind him telling you how you should spend the money, you'll never want for anything.

Head: Incredibly bright, he's a real problem solver and is nothing if not persistent, which is great if he's working on that new room addition, not so great if he's decided the house doesn't need a new addition. You'll never have to ask him to help you around the house. By the time you get up, everything will be done. You'll be begging him for a few more minutes in bed on Sunday morning.

This is a hard-working, high energy, intelligent, not always thoughtful guy. He'll remember your anniversary, but is more likely to buy you a toaster than a teddy.

Heart: Forget about being friends with your ex. He'll have none of that. In fact, forget about being friends with any guy who's not gay. Schnauzer men are extremely jealous and not very sociable, a deadly combination if you're the kind of woman who likes to flirt at parties.

Family: If you have kids with this guy, you'll be taking care of them. He won't be having that "birds and bees" conversation with little Johnny. You will. On the bright side, he won't be bouncing quarters off the bed sheets. A Standard Schnauzer man will insist on seeing the report card, then suggest that you do something about the kid's less than perfect grades.

Work: He enjoys challenges and is bright enough to adapt, but he won't be happy in positions that require constant change. He may be a mathematician, but hasn't the patience of a great teacher. If he's in medicine, you're more likely to find him in research, than standing beside a patient's bed. Many Standard Schnauzer men are happy in business. If he's your boss, don't expect positive reinforcement. When he isn't complaining, you're doing okay. If he's working for you, he'll make you look really good. But be careful, he's ambitious. He might end up with your job.

Best Match with: Professional wives.
Bad Breed for: Free love advocates.

Enough About Me, Let's Talk About Me!
Terriers

TERRIER MEN

The Terrier man is a high-energy, driven, hyperactive, talkative, high-strung go-getter. Fiery, fun and entertaining, he needs lots of attention and can sometimes be downright irritating. A Terrier man loves nothing more than the sound of his own voice. Right or wrong, this guy is on a mission, and if you're unable to understand his mission, you may be left behind. Tenacious to a fault and completely fearless, he's a gung-ho, never-say-die dude. Don't expect to win an argument, as he'll never cave in and he never backs down. If you go for men with gumption (and you don't mind playing the supporting cast to his one-man show), the Terrier may be just the guy for you.

Are you a busy woman, with your own life to lead? Then know that there will be times when the two of you will spend weeks apart, barely passing in the hallway. If you have children, you'll be responsible for the childcare, unless you can afford a nanny. And don't expect your Terrier to be as interested in your work as you are in his. This man is the definition of one-tracked. Only if your work is his work, will you have his undivided attention.

Terriers may be sports-casters, lawyers, campaign managers, gym teachers, actors, activists, entrepreneurs, motivational speakers, anything that keeps them in the limelight or the center ring. He'll have the intelligence and drive to start a successful company, but may lack the diplomacy and people skills to run it once it expands. Famous Terriers? My votes go to James Carville, Ross Perot, Steve Jobs, Jimmy Connors and Ralph Nader.

AIREDALE

Tough and stubborn to the point of insanity, he's the guy on the six o'clock news who is determined to stay with his house during the mudslide. Tune in at eleven? He'll be the guy sliding down the hill in his house. The greatest thing about an Airedale man is that he'll be able to laugh about the whole thing later. He'll be the guy telling the mudslide story at the first party in his rebuilt house, while all your friends split their sides laughing about it. It's hard to believe he's the same guy who was so distant, so aloof in the beginning of your relationship. Maybe he just wanted to make sure you were worthy. It's not so much that he's a snob, he simply knows who he is and what he's looking for in a partner. He won't waste his time on flighty airheads or ditzy broads.

Head: This man is looking for an equal. More attracted by wits than tits, a quick comeback will turn him on faster than a tight teddy. If you can hold your own with him, you'll be in for a wonderful ride.

Heart: Embarrass him or try to control him, he'll seal up his emotions tighter than an Oscar Night envelope. He'll shudder if he hears you say, "We like that," or "Our feeling about it is this..." Make him feel like half of some two-headed monster, he'll detach and run.

Family: His go-all-out attitude may mean that he's not great with newborns and toddlers. You may find yourself reminding him not to throw the baby too high. As much as the Airedale will love his children, he won't be a mushy "tell me what you're feeling" dad. He's more likely to tell the kid to "get over it," or "suck it up."

Work: The guy you send into that big meeting, he never falters under pressure and will bravely walk into the line of fire. He's a proud man, so never berate him. He'll clear out his desk, walk out the door, and never look back. An Airedale man won't work for fools.

> Famous Airedale..?
> Scott McNeely of Sun Microsystems was certainly behaving like a Airedale when he decided to take on Microsoft.

Best Match with: An equal partner, firm but fair.
Bad Breed for: Women who play dumb, submissive types, or ball-busters.

AMERICAN PIT BULL TERRIER
AMERICAN STAFFORDSHIRE TERRIER

Let's be really honest here, a Pit Bull man is not going to be a walk in the doggie park. Because he's both a lover and a fighter, it will take absolutely the right woman to deal with him. If you aren't a completely self-assured person... a person who knows how to put her foot down... don't even consider this man as your life mate. Though he's an excellent judge of character, a Pit Bull man is fiercely protective. The same sweet and utterly charming man who finally won over your mother can turn into

Charles Bronson in "Death Wish" if he sees the mailman smiling at you a little too long. A Pit Bull will stick to you like Velcro. He is suspicious of other men and will not want them anywhere near you. This is not something you can talk him out of. He will not want to hear that Fred was your best friend in college and is just like one of your girlfriends. He will simply want Fred gone. If Fred refuses to go, your Pit Bull is not above knocking him into the next county.

Heart: Relaxing by the fire will not be very relaxing with a Pit Bull. You'll be curled up with your cocoa, he'll be getting up every two minutes to poke the logs or check the flue. If you just can't stand the nightly pacing, tell him you heard something outside and you'll buy yourself several hours of peace. Your Pit Bull will be walking the perimeter of the property with a bat, while you have a leisurely soak in the tub and finish reading two or three of your favorite books.

Head: The Pit Bull doesn't like compromise. Our advice? Speak softly and borrow his bat. You're going to have to lay down the law. Let your rules be known, then stick to them. Never waver. If you can manage that, he can be a teddy bear. Not a rocket scientist, a teddy bear.

Family: How is he with kids? Well... he isn't a "time out" father. He isn't a warm and fuzzy Pop. He's the Hockey Dad who drives his boy to tears every Sunday afternoon... or worse, assaults the Ref for taking his kid out of the game. And it would take a brave young man to ask a Pit Bull's daughter to the prom!

Work: The Pit Bull can figure out how to take a car engine apart, piece by piece, but can't figure out how to make a career out of it. He's going to need some help in the goal department, and it won't be easy to help him. He doesn't much care for advice, whether it comes from you or from another man.

> This is the man you want on your arm if you find yourself in a dark alley, in a bad neighborhood. No one threatens a Pit Bull's loved ones!

Best Match With: Smart, stable, tough-as-nails broads.

Bad Breed for: Teases, wimps, or mean-spirited women.

BORDER TERRIER

He's the Terrier in the plain, brown wrapper. Like Peter Falk's rumple-coated, head-scratching TV detective, "Columbo," he gets the job done, but is never showy about it. The Border Terrier man is "Mr. Understatement" in a world of loud-mouthed, super-charged, "enough about me, let's talk about me" guys. He'd never think of calling attention to himself and, if anything, seems almost self-effacing. If you want Terrier determination, minus the posturing and bravado, try a BT Man. He's honest and hard-working, loving and thoughtful, and while he may not win the beauty contest, he might walk away with the congeniality prize. Very adaptable, he adjusts easily to life in the big city, a small town, or in the country. He's a jeans and sweatshirt guy at home, business casual on the job. Don't ever buy him trendy clothes or try to dress him up. He'll just look like a messy kid on his way to Sunday school.

Heart: Happy and easygoing, a B.T. man will love you unconditionally. He's not too territorial or fussy about his things. What's mine is yours is the Border Terrier's motto. Though not a clingy breed, he'll need lots of physical affection. He'll want to be next to you on the sofa, not across the room in a chair.

Head: Remember to tell him how wonderful he is. Tell him often. Though he seems completely confident, harsh words or nagging can wound him. Anxious to please by nature, he's already hard on himself. When he's made a mistake, he doesn't need you to keep driving home the point. If you do? Be prepared to pay for it. He has a long memory.

If you're the kind of woman who has secrets and wants to keep them, this is not the man for you. He'll notice any change in the normal routine. He's not a jealous lover, nor is he overly possessive, but he'll be miserable if he thinks you're not being truthful with him.

Family: His need to spend time with his family is almost physical. He'll actually feel ill when forced to be away from you. If you and the kids take a trip without him, he'll make his friends and co-workers miserable for the duration. He won't be out pretending he's single; he'll be pitifully staring at the phone with a lukewarm TV dinner in his lap.

Work: The B.T. man is a planner and likes to have all his ducks in a row. A self-starter, he needs a job that combines a routine he can anticipate with interesting challenges. He'd make a great line producer or a team leader for a large project. He doesn't like adversarial relationships with other men and will dismiss aggressive types as idiots. A creative thinker, he excels at work that allows him to solve problems.

Best Match with: Families, love, and attentive partners.
Bad Breed for: Long distance relationships, appearance fanatics.

CAIRN TERRIER

Okay, he's cute like your other Terrier boyfriends, and he's wildly energetic, independent and tough. But don't think you've got this guy pegged. High energy, but not high strung, Cairn men are more relationship oriented than other Terriers. He really needs your attention. Don't try bringing work home from the office if you live with a Cairn. He loves to talk and, unlike most Terriers, not always about himself. He wants to know what you think. He also wants you to be an equal. The Cairn loves a woman who can go toe-to-toe with him. Wimps and doormats won't get to a second date. Sweet and cuddly though he may be, he's also territorial. Like a companion dog on steroids, one minute he's cuddled up with you on the couch, the next he's facing down some guy who glanced at you in the movie ticket line. Except for close friends, his relationships with other men are combative.

Head: In his mind, he's the size of a Wolfhound, so it's likely that you'll spend some time tending to his battle scars. All the will in the world won't help him when he confronts a guy twice his size, and believe us, he will. Get yourself a really good medical plan or stay away from situations that could bring out his jealous nature.

Heart: You'll never have to guess how he feels about things. A Cairn man lets you know in no uncertain terms. The trade off for those deeply personal fireside communions will be the incessant grumbling you'll have to listen to when he's had a bad day. Most women think he's worth it.

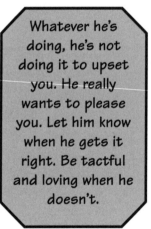

Whatever he's doing, he's not doing it to upset you. He really wants to please you. Let him know when he gets it right. Be tactful and loving when he doesn't.

Family: The Cairn loves taking the family on outings and, after a busy day, he wants nothing more than to pile up on the couch with you and the kids. If there is friction in the family, it will be because someone has used a tool and not replaced it, or has destroyed his favorite CD. He'll probably need a room of his own where he can keep his things.

Work: The Cairn is unlikely to have a physical job. He's a solution man. Cooperative enough to work with a team, he is more productive in a leadership position, or a job outside of the hierarchy. The Cairn is territorial and won't like others… especially other men… edging into his designated area. Look for him in jobs connected with new technologies, in research and development, or in marketing. He won't, however, be a true geek. He's too much of a people person to qualify for that title.

Best Match with: Pollyannas, equal partners.
Bad Breed for: Withholders, silent types, those who need a quiet household.

FOX TERRIER

If you like to watch the political pundits on those Sunday morning talk shows, you have surely seen James Carville aggressively defending his friend, Bill Clinton, or aggressively attacking some unlucky conservative. You have? Then you've seen the archetypal Fox Terrier man in action. Lucky for Mary Matalin, and other partners of Fox Terrier men, this breed has its flip side. For every lunge at the throat, there's a moment of incredible fun. For every pointed barb, there's the hysterical joke. He can be feisty and charming, buoyantly happy and impossibly stubborn, all in the same moment. If nothing else, he's the guy that you pray is on your team... the man for whom the word "scrappy" was invented. He is scrappy incarnate... the master of scrap.

Heart: He's the kid on the basketball court who throws himself into the bleachers on the non-existent chance that he might get the ball back for his team. He will do this even if his team is winning 105 to 27 with one minute remaining in the game. He's the kid you rush to the emergency room because he's just tried to defend his little brother against five larger and older school bullies. He got two of them, but the other three beat the tar out of him.

Head: Incredibly bright, insatiably curious. When a Fox Terrier child asks, "Why?" God help you if you don't explain things to his satisfaction. You'd better have the full answer to his question along with indisputable documentation from assorted historians, scholars, and experts. If not, cancel your dinner plans. You're going to be there for awhile.

Family: Loyal and protective, a devoted father and loving mate. Still, his large personality may be overwhelming for young children. Thanks to his tendency to rant when irritated, you may find yourself having to say, "Not so loud, dear, you're upsetting the children."

Work: His mind is large enough to take in all the possibilities and sharp enough to focus on the job that needs doing. Once he's focused, you'd do well to get out of his way.

Best Match with: Tough cookies, like minds.
Bad Breed For: Marshmallows, the easily exhausted.

JACK RUSSELL TERRIER

He's the friend who convinced you to pull your savings out of money market funds so that he could make you millions with his E-Trade ability. You now have no savings, a lot of

Priceline.com stock, and an autographed glossy of William Shatner. Suddenly, you're hoarding sleeping pills and fantasizing about painful ways you can take him out with you. What were you thinking? He seemed so sure of himself. He was so convincing and so damned cocky. He's still cocky. It wasn't his fault. The only problem is that you ran out of money. If you could just come up with another five grand, he could get it all back with interest. Buckets of interest. And he's probably right. He is, after all, a Jack Russell.

Head: He's the smartest guy you've ever met, but he's so crazy that it hardly matters. He's the most inter- esting guy you've ever met, but you're so exhausted you're no longer able to appreciate it. And if you think you can train him, get over yourself now. He's onto you before you can say "heel" and will have you trained in a matter of days.

FYI...
The world actually *does* revolve around him!

Heart: Yes, he loves you and wants to be with you, but it can sometimes feel like you're more of a chauffeur than a partner. You spend half your time in the emergency room, having him patched up. He's provoked a grudge match with your neighbor Raphael, the world kickboxing champion. He loves to mouth off in biker bars. He goes to out-of-town games just so he can heckle the hometown fans.

Family: He's better at entertaining other people's kids than he is at living with kids of his own. The problem? He competes with them. He competes with them for your time and attention.

He competes with them for the last piece of fried chicken. He competes with them for the television remote. He will never let Little Jimmy beat him in a wrestling match. Little Jimmy's only four and already needs therapy.

Work: The Jack Russell doesn't follow his bliss. He doesn't have bliss, he has drive, and he doesn't follow anything, he attacks it with a vengeance. The man's like a human cannonball. Just point him at a target and he'll get there. He'll get there yesterday. The target is history. Point him at the wrong target, he's happy to destroy it, too. He never frets about the moral implications. He just goes. This man needs to work alone and will get crazy if he's not allowed to control his environment. What's the worst possible work situation for a JR? Stick him in a small office cubicle with a guy just like him. What you'll get is "Dilbert in Thunderdome." Two Jacks may enter, but only one Jack leaves.

Best Match with: Really secure women, wild chicks, saints
Bad Breed For: Attention seekers, the faint of heart

SCOTTISH TERRIER

We recently visited the home of a friend who has a house full of boys. We were having coffee in her breakfast nook, as her husband and three sons sat on the living room floor, arguing loudly, while trying to assemble a home entertainment center. Humorous insults and derisive laughter filled the house. Every single thing these males said to each other could be boiled down to the following simple statement: "I'm great and you're not." They were all Scottish Terriers. Don't get me wrong. The Scottie is a lovable guy and is, for the most part, sensible and good-tempered. It's just that his relationships with other men tend to be combative. This can be a good thing. Give him regular nights out with the boys and he won't feel the need to "bark" at you!

Heart: He will run the gamut of every possible emotional state during almost every single day. Don't take his mood swings personally. His temperament is biologically determined, spelled out in his genes. There's nothing you can do, or stop doing, that will change him.

> A Tip... Never give your Scottie an ultimatum: "Be at little Johnny's game or I'm leaving you." He won't be there and you'll have to put up or shut up.

Head: His mind is always whirring. Try not to complain that he spends too much time at work. He's happiest working and so is less likely to put you through one of his moods.

Family: He loves his kids, but he doesn't understand that the four-year-old won't start closing the front door the first time (or even the fiftieth time) you tell her. He'll think she's a little slow and may start treating her that way. The fact that he's a workaholic means that, yes... he's the dad who'll miss the school play or the last soccer game of the season.

Work: It's no accident that a high percentage of American millionaires are men of Scottish ancestry. The Scottie is a bulldozer, pushy and goal-oriented. While not a wildly creative type, he has the smarts to envision his goal, the common sense to make it a reality and the drive to see it through to the end. You will never starve with this man on the job.

Best Match with: Thick-skinned women, the easily bored.
Bad Breed for: Doormats, co-dependents, thin-skinned partners.

SOFT-COATED WHEATEN TERRIER

At last! A man with all that Terrier drive, who doesn't make you want to shoot him halfway through the second date. High-spirited and fun loving, the Wheatie man is less aggressive and quick-tempered than most Terriers. He's also more sociable, a real people person. You won't have to worry about him dragging home strays. You may, however, have to go fetch him when someone else has dragged him off. The genial Wheatie could get caught up in a conversation at the market while you're sitting home waiting for your cold medicine. Don't send him on a quick errand if you've only got one car and an important business meeting in forty-five minutes. He won't make it, you won't make it, and neither of you will have sex for months over it.

Head: His curiosity tends to get the best of him, he frequently follows his nose into trouble, and he's fearless to his own detriment. Remind him that wandering out at midnight to investigate a strange noise may not be wise. Calmly suggest that following a suspicious looking car full of hoodlums might not be prudent. Quietly explain why it's better to make sure the water is deep enough before he dives off the quarry wall.

Heart: The tip of his tie always seems to end up in the soup. His shoes always seem to need polishing. And for heaven's sake, don't let him order spaghetti at a business dinner! As for his wardrobe, you're going to have to dress him. Get used to repeating the phrase, "You're not going to wear that, are you?" Lucky for you, the Wheatie cleans up nicely. But he'll never understand why the green tie is ugly or why you feel ill when he wears the brown suit.

Family: He'll take an active parenting role and will love showing off his kids. Keep in mind, however, that he will go to the office with spit-up on his shirt. There will be the faint scent of baby poop on his suit coat. Do him a favor and give him the once over before he heads out the door for that big meeting.

Work: The Wheatie man has the energy and drive to run for public office, but would want to stick to the issues rather than run a "down and dirty" campaign. Once in office, he'll remain steady and strong, showing up for every vote, picking his battles wisely, refusing to toe the party line. In our opinion, Senator John McCain could well be one of this breed. The Wheatie is smart and full of creative ideas. Should he invent a better mousetrap, he'll also manufacture it, market it, wrap it in a box and drive it to UPS. Still, he's no Bill Gates. He'll try to outsell his competitors, but he won't try to obliterate them.

Best Match with: A no-nonsense partner, one who shares his vision.
Bad Breed for: Neatniks, superficial types.

WEST HIGHLAND WHITE TERRIER

There's an idea going around that intelligence equates with cynicism. The smarter you are, the more likely you are to suspect the motives of your fellow humans. Anyone who believes this has never met a Westie. Not only is he highly intelligent, he's bouncy, joyous and fun... a natural optimist. He lives to play and is more sociable with strangers than others in the Terrier group. Anything you can do outside that involves dirty is a great thing. He's creative, smart as a whip, and tends to get so excited about his current project that he works himself into a manic state. Thanks to his high energy level and active mind, he may suffer from insomnia. During periods of over-excitement and little sleep, he may become testy and snappish. Help him establish a cut-off point in the evening, pour him a glass of wine and encourage him to relax. You'll be doing yourself and him a favor.

Heart: He's definitely not a fighter, but he can occasionally be irritable. And while he may love you to the ends of the earth, don't expect him to love everybody you love. The really good news is he doesn't need constant reassurance or pampering from you. Not that he doesn't enjoy it, he just won't fall apart without it.

Head: The Westie is a man with strong opinions. He can be stubborn and uncooperative, if he gets his back up. If you want him to consider your point of view, it's best to come around the side door, not hit him with it head-on.

Family: He's a playful, fun-loving dad. But this is not a man who can hide his feelings. He may favor one family member over another and this will be evident.

Work: He's energetic and self-reliant, a real problem solver. He may be an inventor. Or he might be a scientist, probably working toward some real-life goal... tracking down that disease-causing gene and figuring out how to disarm it. This man does not give up easily. If the job takes a year, fine. If it takes several decades, well... that's how long it takes. Once he's on a mission he'll go through hell and high water to complete it.

Best Match with: Busy, social partners.
Bad Breed for: Control freaks, overly dignified partners.

Please Toy With My Affections...
Companion Dogs

COMPANION DOG MEN

Attention coddling Cathies, pampering Peggies and doting Debbies! Have I got a man for you! Not only will he rub your feet while you're cuddled up, watching "Sleepless in Seattle," your Companion Dog Man actually likes "Sleepless in Seattle." He's sweet, he's loving and he's a real homebody. More than anything else, he'll need a lot of love and a lot of attention from you. Sometimes low maintenance, sometimes a royal pain in the rear, this is a man who prefers the indoors to the outdoors. Whatever his temperament, get used to the fact that he'll be in the house with you. So while I can't guarantee quality time, I can promise you quantity time.

Excelling in jobs that require intelligence and concentration, Companion Dog Men often choose careers as bookkeepers, illustrators, librarians, technical writers, and home catalog businessmen. Don't expect a celebrity. Companion Dog Men aren't likely to seek the limelight and, excluding the few with Terrier traits, men in this group rarely become famous. Generally speaking, Companion Dog Men are likely to either be shy and retiring, or high-strung and dependent.

Like the toy dogs, which were bred to be pleasant company for their owners, most Companion Dog Men are happier in a two-way relationship than in a family with lots of kids. If you dream of finding a good man and starting a home-based business, there may be a Companion Dog in your future. Bob Newhart's Innkeeper, from the old Bob Newhart Show, is definitely one of this type.

As a rule, Companion Dog Men hate to be yelled at or bossed. If you bully them, they can become "shy-sharp" and may snap at you. And not all members of the Companion Group are sweet-natured and quiet. Some are quite pushy. You've probably had a run-in with a Companion Dog Man who didn't know when to shut up and when to back down.

BRUSSELS GRIFFON

I'll give you the bad news first. He's high-strung, demanding, thin-skinned, and stubborn. He can be unpredictable, even neurotic. He's a picky eater and will stand behind you, offering well-meaning advice, as you're cooking a meal. He'll not only order his salad dressing on the side but will want assurances that the olive oil used in the dressing is cold pressed. If he's not satisfied with his food once it gets to him, he'll send it back. And, as he probably suffers from allergies, he may wheeze and snore. Think Felix Ungar, from "The Odd Couple." Now for the good news... He's very bright, very busy, and never boring. He's probably college educated and is certainly well-read. If he sees something he wants, he goes after it with Terrier-like tenacity. Less of a homebody than many in the Companion Dog group, he has no problem negotiating his way around the outside world. If you enjoy flea markets, estate sales, or street fairs, know that your Griffon man will be off and running before you can put the car in park. He will not wait for you to catch up.

Heart: He loves to talk with you about the books you've read and the movies you've seen. Usually attracted to city life, you're much more likely to find him window shopping on Madison Avenue, than fly-fishing in Montana.

Head: This man is a really good judge of character and you can rely on his instincts. A Griffon pal once saved my entire circle of friends from investing in a land deal being promoted by a charming acquaintance. "I don't trust that guy," was the Griff's constant mantra, "He smiles too much and I really hate that purple power tie." While the rest of us were cashing in our mutual fund shares, our Griffon buddy had uncovered the fact that this man had pulled the same scam on some folks in another city.

Family: The Griffon will be okay with kids, but they aren't his first priority. He'll be a better dad once they're older. And he'll want a social life that doesn't include them. He enjoys the theatre and the opera. He'd rather see a drama with a good cast, than a big guns, special effects movie... or certainly any film that features mice in big, white gloves.

Work: Though he's extroverted enough to have a job out in the big bad world, he isn't cooperative enough to work as a member of a team. He might be a newspaper columnist, or a restaurant or theatre critic. He may be an architect, or an antique dealer. As he's a good judge of value, you may find him appraising jewelry. Other Griffons can be found on college faculties, usually in the literature or arts departments.

Best Match with: Cultured, urban women. Intellectuals.
Bad Breed for: Cowgirls, outdoorsy types, clinging vines, or Plain Janes.

CAVALIER KING CHARLES SPANIEL

While everyone loves a Cav, not everyone should be with him. He's attractive because he's a happy, enthusiastic, in-the-moment, constantly smelling the roses kind of guy. He won't be a big money earner and he won't push you to be one. "There are more important things than money!" you may be saying to yourself. True. But if neither of you is making money, all the hugs and cuddles in the world won't matter when the repo man shows up to drag your car away. And if you're the kind of woman who needs a gentle push or a pep talk once in awhile, you won't get it from a Cav. If it's Sunday morning and you haven't finished that big presentation for Monday, don't look to him for inspiration. He's more likely to suggest that you work too hard and that a day at the beach might be fun.

> For a high-strung, highly stressed, high blood pressure woman, a Cav Man is like walking Valium. My pal Helen, for instance, is a successful entrepreneur married to a laid-back Cav. He tends the garden, cooks the meals, coaches the kids' soccer team, and rubs her shoulders at the end of a long day. For her, it's a match made in heaven

Heart: He's a huggable, easy-going, sweetheart of a man, who'll happily join you on your morning run, or cuddle with you in front of your favorite tear-jerker. A Cav man hates spending too much time alone and may grumble and moan if he feels he's not getting enough attention.

Head: Did I say "in the moment?" Like his canine counterpart, your Cav man will chase a ball right into the path of an oncoming car.

Family: This man is a mellow soul, he's cooperative, loves his family, and makes a wonderful dad. Your Mom is crazy about him, your friends want to steal him, and the kids next door want him to come out and play. Though he's agile and athletic, you're more likely to find him playing Frisbee with his kids, than knocking heads with his buddies on the rugby field.

Work: He's not boss material, and is happy to accept others as leaders. Give him a time to be there and a job to do, he'll be there on time and he'll do the job. Left to his own devices, he may fritter away an entire day without really getting started on anything. Don't look for the Cav in jobs where deadlines are a priority. You might find him working as a masseur, a physical therapist, or high school counselor. He'd make a great partner in a Mom & Pop business, as long as Mom's there to keep him on track.

Best Match with: Affectionate, demonstrative, self-motivated partners.
Bad Breed for: Control freaks, Lady MacBeth types, Helpless Hannahs.

CHIHUAHUA

He yells at the television news, calls to complain about plans for a new strip mall, writes, emails, and faxes everyone with whom he has a beef. He can frequently be seen purchasing "no trespassing" signs at the hardware store. If he's not careful, he could become a constant litigator, at the expense of his work and his relationships. If you're involved with this man, plan fun activities to help distract him from the hundred or so injustices he's fighting. My neighbor's Chihuahua husband is very possessive of his things. Everything must be in its place before he can relax. He's often heard voicing a disapproving opinion on someone's choice of clothing or hairstyle. He's usually the first to point out that someone else is driving poorly.

Head: He's extremely bright, terribly alert, and needs to keep his fertile mind occupied. He's almost too curious and bold, always leaping before looking. While some accuse him of not being able to "shut his yap", others see him as a courageous activist.

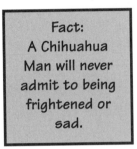

Fact:
A Chihuahua Man will never admit to being frightened or sad.

Heart: The Chihuahua man tends to be clannish, preferring to stay with his chosen group. This trait may cause others (known to the Chihuahua as "those people") to speculate that he's anti-social. Encourage him to socialize with people outside of his circle. He'll be better for it.

Family: Thanks to his thin-skinned temperament, crying infants and active young children may bring out his snappish and irritable side. You'll need to constantly remind him that children do better when given both positive reinforcement and a sunny view of the world around them.

Work: The Chihuahua would make a wonderful newspaper reporter. Once he's onto a story, he'll keep asking questions until he gets at the truth. He'd be an effective lobbyist for a cause he believes in. Any government official would be tempted to give him his vote, just to get the Chihuahua off his back. On the darker end of the spectrum, this man could be a member of the paparazzi, relentlessly stalking his famous prey.

Best Match with: Activists.
Bad Breed for: "Don't Rock the Boat" types.

ITALIAN GREYHOUND

If you ask an I.G. man about his childhood, he will regale you with well-worn stories of how he was mercilessly bullied in the schoolyard and picked on in gym class. He was the child the other kids would tell you was "beggin' to be beat up." A true introvert, he's intimidated by the outside world... and with good reason. Given a choice, he'll always prefer flight to fight. As an adult, he can be unpredictable and is likely to be neurotic and unstable. Get used to the feel of icy feet in bed. I.G's are cold natured and will require extra blankets and a non-drafty house. He's also sensitive to outside stimuli and would much rather attend a wine tasting than a kegger. Think Niles Crane of the TV show, "Frazier."

Head: You don't have to worry about the I.G. dumping you in favor of his buddies on a Saturday night. He doesn't have a lot of male friends. When you tell your male friends you're dating him, be prepared for the response, "Really? Wow! I thought he was gay." Other men just don't get this guy. He will fit nicely in your writers' group or in an acting class, but don't expect him to blend in at a sports bar or on a construction site.

Heart: On the bright side, there are plenty of women out there who prefer sensitive to macho. He's not possessive, he's very cooperative, and he won't try to boss you around. The Italian Greyhound man won't give you much trouble. And though he won't protect you from burglars or lonely drunks in bars, he can be quite affectionate with a woman he's come to trust. If you're looking for a pet in partner's clothing, this may be your man.

Family: The Italian Greyhound may be too high-strung and thin-skinned for some kids. He's definitely not a rough and tumble Pop. Girly-girls and quiet boys will adore him. Future Sports Hall of Fame inductees will be a bit embarrassed on father-son night.

Work: While he's alert, learns fast, and has the energy needed to perform well in the working world, his nervous temperament can get in his way. His ongoing battle with his own neuroses may cause him to be attracted to the field of psychiatry. Unfortunately, his own neuroses may keep him from being a good psychiatrist. As he'll know every mental disturbance in the book, he's an excellent diagnostician, but may lack the empathy necessary to be truly helpful.

Best Match with: Women into role-reversal, extreme caretakers.

Bad Breed for: Outdoorsy types, women with "white knight" complexes.

JAPANESE CHIN

He's a lover, not a fighter, a wonderful companion and a sensitive mate. A Chin man is a born optimist. Full of fun, playful and happy, this guy loves to perform. Because he's naturally observant and cooperative, a Chin will adapt to your lifestyle quickly. Unless your idea of bliss is roughing it in the wilderness, you'll never have to "train" him. A Chin likes comfort and won't be fun on a camp-out. His idea of a perfect vacation is a luxury hotel, room service, and long, well-shaded naps on the beach. You'll love taking him to parties and social affairs because he knows how to dress and when to exit gracefully. Chin men always look good, always say the right things, and never overstay their welcome.

Heart: Mr. Chin needs a close relationship. Very close. You may have to stop him from following you into the bath. He's easily wounded and never forgets a slight. It's not so much that he holds a grudge. Life's too short for that. He just treats the offender like a tumor that he's cut out of his life.

Head: The Chin Man is exceedingly bright and lets you know, in no uncertain terms, what he likes and dislikes. One thing he dislikes is messiness. He will not abide clutter in his home, business, or car.

Family: He's not adverse to fatherhood and will make a fine dad for a kid in the chess club, but might have a hard time with aggressive children. Like others of the Companion Group, he won't understand a junior jock and will not enjoy wrestling or physical games.

> The Chin can become so wrapped up his work that he completely loses all track of time. Remind him to eat. If he gets involved with something, he may forget and he suffers from low blood sugar. If he suffers, you'll suffer!

Work: As the saying goes, people are either paid for what they do, or for what they know. The Chin gets paid for what he knows. He's the medical expert who gets called to testify in court. He's the authority on Pre-Colombian art, hired by a museum to appraise a new find. If he's a musician, he's probably classical (never grunge or hard rock) and may be a composer or conductor.

Best Match with: A close, loving, gentle partner.
Bad Breed for: Jocks, women who want a project.

MALTESE

He always brings a bottle of wine to a dinner, or a gift to the party's hostess. He moves through the room, paying compliments to the ladies and kissing hands. He's an utterly charming fellow with an impish grin and a sparkle in his eye. He's an asset to any gathering, as he's able to converse on a diverse array of subjects, from politics to popular novels. He knows all the juicy gossip. Still, he won't want to travel outside of his usual circles. If he feels that people around him are not his intellectual equals, he may subtly torture them with references and jokes that are over their heads. There is a bit of the devil in this angelic man. Encourage him to socialize outside his sphere. Many Maltese men come from wealthy, cultured families. These men don't have to work, but it's a bad thing if they don't. A Maltese needs new challenges and contact with new people, to keep him from settling into neurosis and dependency.

Head: The Maltese man is well spoken and quite intelligent. If he isn't college educated, he can "pass." Though cultured and refined, he is not high-strung or timid.

Heart: Gentle and well-mannered, he won't mind sitting in silence with you, reading a good book or just listening to the summer night. And while he's no macho man, he manages, all the same, to be bold and vigorous. Trusting, affectionate, and playful, the Maltese makes a lovely life partner.

Family: This is not a man who really desires fatherhood. Children just aren't interesting to him. They're messy and noisy and far too much trouble. Presented with the hard, cold fact of a pregnancy, he may not react well. But don't despair, he'll probably come around. He'll enjoy the kids once he can sit down with them and have a conversation. Be aware that Maltese men are quicker to dismiss than inquire.

> Warning!
> You may suggest to this man... you may coax, bribe, wheedle, convince, or tempt him. But do not push. He will become irritable and snap at you.

Work: He'll be attracted to jobs that require the use of his intellect and will only be happy when he gets the attention he feels he deserves. A Maltese has wonderful taste and will be drawn to the arts, though his love of the good life could prevent him from actually becoming an artist. He's more likely to be an art critic or the owner of an art gallery. He may manage a theatre company or own a vineyard. He would be successful in the world of publishing. Whatever he does, he does well.

Best Match with: Cultured, educated women.
Bad Breed for: Hoot and Holler gals, Old Mother Hubbards.

MINIATURE PINSCHER

Some years ago, I took a driving course, having let my license lapse after several carless years in Manhattan. Two men in the class captured my interest. One was a strapping, young "working dog" type, recently returned from having served with the Marines in Desert Storm. He was happy, secure, and had nothing to prove to himself or anyone else. The other young man was one of those intense, pushy, leg-humping little guys… too macho for his size (or because of it)… who had been ordered by the court to take the class. When asked to tell the class why he was there, he rattled off a list that included speeding violations, running red lights, reckless driving, and driving with a suspended license. By the tone in his voice, you could tell not only was he unrepentant, he was proud of his reckless behavior! Unlike the former Marine, he had everything to prove and he was proving it with his car. He was certainly a Miniature Pinscher.

Head: He smokes cigars while you're eating. He cuts in front of you in line. If he doesn't know you, or you can't do something for him, you're not important. We know what you're thinking. "He can't be all bad!" Well, you're right. The Min Pin has lots of style. He's entertaining, lively, and smart as a whip. Completely self-possessed, he has what theatre critics call "stage presence." If you can live with the rest of the package, he'll make sure you're never bored.

Heart: All the qualities that make the Min Pin dog funny and entertaining, make the Min Pin man a royal pain in the rear. Extremely territorial, Mr. Min Pin's attitude can be summed up as, "Don't get in my space, don't touch my things, don't speak to the woman I was thinking about approaching." The angry character, Paul Lazzaro, from Kurt Vonnegut's "Slaughter House Five" and Joe Peshi's belligerent Tommy in "Goodfellas" were extreme examples of the Min Pin personality gone terribly wrong.

Family: Please do not inflict the Min Pin on children. He's the kind of dad who makes for lots of therapy and many years of blame.

Work: If he's the boss, he drives everyone crazy. If he's an employee, he drives his boss crazy. If he's a co-worker, try sending ill-gotten copies of his resume to other companies.
Whether he's in his car, his shower, or sitting across the dinner table from you, he's glued to his cell phone. And yes, that is his phone that keeps going off in the middle of the movie. Min Pins are often attracted to the business side of Hollywood, where you'll find them as television and movie studio executives. If they live on the East Coast, they're usually trial lawyers or car salesmen.

Best Match with: Those who crave trouble.
Bad Breed for: The easily irritated, the easily embarrassed

PAPILLON

Look out onto any neighborhood baseball diamond, basketball court, or soccer field and you'll notice him right away. There! That little guy with the huge heart, incredibly alert, completely into the game. All during his childhood, his parents will watch nervously from the sidelines as their diminutive son attempts to tackle players twice his size. The crowd holds its collective breath until the Papillon kid rises from the bottom of the pile, unhurt and more determined than ever. After the game, bruised and battered, the Papillon boy will focus on nothing but the next game. This tremendous focus extends into adulthood.

Heart: When you're with him, you feel that you're the only woman in the world! He makes you want to do things for him and he, in return, would give you the shirt off his back. At a party, he's just as likely to be found in the kitchen, chatting with the gals, as talking sports with the guys on the patio.

WARNING!
The Papillon has a tendency to become dependent on his partner.

Head: At his best, he's engaging and entertaining… at his worst, an incessant talker and borderline yappy. Intelligent and cooperative, he can also be moody and inconsistent. He's often eccentric and can develop odd little quirks and habits. If you're a dedicated conformist, this could be a problem.

Family: While he's a better father than most Companion Men, fatherhood is not his first priority. Remind him that children don't respond well to being talked to death. A simple "pick up your shoes," repeated until the request is complied with, works better than a long lecture on the virtues of cleanliness.

Work: With his excellent mind and a phenomenal attention span, he's well suited for fields that require study or long preparation. He won't go for jobs that require him to scratch and claw his way to the top. He likes people too much and doesn't enjoy beating up on the other guy. His "win-win" philosophy could make him a great negotiator.

Best Match with: An equal partner, Chatty Cathies.
Bad Breed for: Women who need a keeper.

PEKINGESE

Who's that man in the beautifully tailored tux, laughing politely as he skewers a nearby guest with his razor tongue? Condescending and, at the same time, absolutely charming, he's at the top of the guest list for all the best parties. Famous for his brilliant jibes and sarcastic witticisms, the Pekingese rivals Oscar Wilde in the bon mot department. A hostess would never want to slight him. He might turn his famous talent on her! This is not a man to take "slumming" down at the country-western bar. He can't pass for an average guy and trying to

153

adjust to the unfamiliar surroundings will simply tie his stomach in a knot. After all, what's the fun of insulting someone who doesn't understand they've been insulted?

Head: Self-important and exasperatingly hardheaded, the only thing larger than his vocabulary is his opinion of himself. As far as our Peke is concerned, anything that he doesn't know really isn't worth knowing. Like an iron fist in a velvet glove, he can bend the most hard-nosed adversary to his will.

Heart: Quite demanding, this aristocratic gentleman has been known to turn on those closest to him, if he feels he's not getting his fair share of attention. Peke men tend to guard their belongings jealously and have a "what's mine is mine and what's yours is mine" attitude. He would never give you the shirt off his back. He won't even let you borrow it!

Family: As a husband and father, the Pekingese makes a wonderful acquaintance. Entertaining and always good for a fun evening, he's like the much-treasured heirloom necklace that one only takes out on special occasions. This man is not for everyday wear.

Work: His motto might be: "If you want something done right, hire the best and order them around." He's the antique dealer, overseeing a workshop packed with refinishers, refurbishers, and polishers. He's the historian, collecting information about his favorite period, just as he collects military belt buckles. He's the curator of an art museum, but will never be an artist. A life with no safety net would be terrifying for the Pekingese.

Best Match for: The woman who simply needs a charming escort.
Bad Breed for: Waking up with in the morning.

POMERANIAN

If you're past a certain age, you may remember Samantha Stevens' busybody neighbor, Gladys Kravitz, from the old "Bewitched" TV show. Perhaps, if you're younger, you've caught Gladys snooping on TV LAND or NICK AT NIGHT. Gladys is always peeking between the curtains, knocking on her neighbor's door, or staring through binoculars to see what was going on across the street. Curious to a fault, the Pomeranian man is male Gladys Kravitz. Undaunted and sharp-tempered, the Pom is hardly what you might describe as "sweet." You might better describe him as "peppery." He loves to talk and has opinions on every subject. It's a good thing he's bright, or this trait might prove tiring. Precisely because he is so bright, he's immensely entertaining, and always keeps you on your toes. He's the perfect match for the woman who loves to argue for argument's sake. In fact, he needs a woman who's not afraid to give him back some of what he dishes out.

Heart: Whether dashing for the train in the morning, or charging down an office corridor, this is a man who loves to run. If you let him, he'll run all over you. You must stand firm. In fact, stand in front of the bathroom mirror and practice saying, "Don't be ridiculous," and "You must think I'm an idiot."

Alternately, you can sit behind a newspaper and practice muttering, "That's nice," and "You don't say?" in a detached, Abner Kravitz way.

Head: Obviously absent for the "sharing is good" lesson in kindergarten, a Pom will guard his personal possessions like a dragon's horde of gold. His big mouth often gets him into trouble. He will spout off just as loudly when talking to a drunken Marine as he does to the six-year-old who kicked a ball into his yard. Not a good idea for a man whose idea of a workout is opening a bottle of wine with a cheap corkscrew.

Family: The Pomeranian man has very little tolerance for children and isn't what you would call gentle with them. He doesn't hate children. He just doesn't understand the point of them. They take attention away from him, mess up his house, touch his things and are just plain irritating most of the time.

Work: The Pom is no yes man, so don't hire him if you're looking for affirmation that your every idea is golden. And don't expect the Pom to quietly follow orders. He'd be unhappy and you'd be wasting his talent. He's best in jobs where boldness and independence of thought are assets. Put him in marketing, or research and development. Any job that allows him to flex his snoop muscle will also be fine. He'll make a wonderful gossip columnist.

Best Match with: Thick-skinned, sarcastic gals, female "Abner Kravitz" types.

Bad Breed for: The easily wounded, anyone who liked "The Waltons".

TOY POODLE

Like Ingrid Bergman's Victor in the movie Casablanca, this is an extremely brilliant man, who must be taken care of absolutely. In fact, the Toy Poodle man is the brightest of all the Companions who, as a group, are unusually bright. He is always willing to cooperate... as long as he's getting what he needs... which is only every ounce of your time and energy. He may sulk or nag, if not given the required attention. If nagging doesn't work, he may become irritable or passive-aggressive. You leave for a weekend and come home to find the place completely trashed because he was looking for "that book" and couldn't find it.

Head: Though it is possible to find stable examples of the Toy Poodle Man, the extreme type is quite phobic. He may try to quiet his brilliant mind with alcohol or pills. He might exhibit compulsive behavior. He may be hypersexual, indulging in numerous affairs or disappearing from the marital bed each night to view sex videos in the privacy of his den. Or he may be completely asexual, finding his bliss only in reading, work, or religion.

Heart: If you need a man to listen intently to your problems and help you through your bad days, get yourself a shrink. Pour your gut out to him and your TP man will simply stare at you with an expression that says, "What does any of this have to do with me?"

> "So what do I get out of this relationship?" you may well ask. He looks great on your arm when you go out for the evening. He's an interesting companion. His conversation never bores. Your heart sings when he turns that loving gaze on you and melts when he falls asleep with his head on your lap. Only a selfish woman could ask for more!

Family: The Toy Poodle man does not want children. He is the child. Oddly, this is the very quality that makes him so extremely attractive to so many women. In the presence of the Toy Poodle man, the maternal instinct leaps forward to meet the challenge. "He needs me! He really, really needs me!"

Work: Don't look for this man at a construction site or on a football field. He won't be there. He'll be the guy in the lab coat hunched over a microscope, or the sleep-deprived programmer awash in the blue glow of the computer screen. You may meet him in the university lecture hall, or find him listening to radio waves for signs of intelligent life on other worlds. Just tie his shoes for him, make sure he gets his meals, lay out his clothing the night before, and all will be right with the world.

Best Match with: Childless Mommies.
Bad Breed for: Adult children.

PUG

My old, southern grandmother, God bless her soul, was never a big fan of sex. The highest praise she ever had for any man was, "He doesn't bother his wife much." She would've loved a man like the Pug. If you've been badly burned in your previous relationships and tend to think all men are too much trouble, let me introduce you to Mr. Pug. This man is no trouble at all. Clean cut and positive, he's an easygoing fellow, always polite, always pleasant. He complies with the laws of his country and state. He needs very little, and won't expect his woman to coddle or wait on him.

Heart: As a lover, the Pug makes a good friend. As a matter of fact, he's heard the old saw "let's just be friends" from more ex-girlfriends than you can imagine. Amazingly enough, he's still friends with all of them. That's the kind of guy he is.

Head: Perfect for the slightly bossy woman, he lets you control the TV remote, pick the restaurant, choose the movie, and decorate the house any way you want. Just be sure you temper your need to be the Alpha. Mr. Pug, easygoing as he may be, does possess a stubborn side. If he feels you've crossed the control line, you could find yourself in a battle. After all, a guy can only give in so much before he has to put his paw down.

Besides, where are you going to find another man this stable and easy to live with?

Family: The Pug man is good with children and makes a loving, consistent parent. He may not understand an eccentric child... an artist, a brainy kid, or a child who is gay. He's just too normal. But he'll love them just the same.

Work: His performance in this arena is much like his performance in the bedroom... unremarkable. He's a steady, stable fellow who will probably make a living but will never set the world on fire. He won't be a salesman. He's not pushy enough. A job in police work or fire-fighting would be too macho an endeavor for a guy this mellow. Whatever he does, his co-workers will like him. He has a good sense of humor and will never try to take their jobs. His boss will like him because he's consistent and not a troublemaker. Look for him in jobs that require stability and practicality... nothing too creative and definitely nothing dangerous. Dry cleaning? Hardware store employee? Librarian? Notary Public? Bank teller? Got the idea?

Best Match with: Homebodies, cuddlers
Bad Breed for: Peak experience junkies, wave-makers

SHIH TZU

He'll run your bath and pour you a glass of wine while you wind down from your hectic day. He's a good listener... a lover, buddy and therapist, rolled into one. A cuddly, cooperative, compassionate mate, the Shih Tzu man is truly woman's best friend.

Head: He's the kind of man that other men don't always understand. For one thing, he doesn't speak "Guy Talk." Endless conversations about sports teams will bore him to tears. His vocabulary includes words like "felicitous" and "prerogative." An aristocrat to the marrow, his demeanor may seem haughty to those who don't know him.

Heart: He has a great sense of humor and enjoys making people laugh as much as he enjoys making them think. He won't mind sharing everything he has with you. Though he can be quite stubborn at times, he's not a fighter and will rarely lose his temper. Stable and reliable, you won't have to worry about him staying out all night, or forgetting to pay the electric bill.

Family: The Shih Tzu man is a natural with kids. He's not a Little League Dad but will enjoy camping, swimming, hiking, and playing tennis with his kids. He'll love helping them with their homework. And when they're feeling blue, he'll listen to their problems, wipe their tears away and them make them laugh with his best Jim Carey impersonation.

Work: He's not competitive, yet he needs to feel like the king of his own domain. He'll almost certainly have a low-key job that, nevertheless, allows him to play the expert. If he's a teacher, you're more likely to find him in a small college than in a large university. He hates faculty politics and enjoys being the big fish in his small pond. He'll probably be a history professor, or maybe teach medieval literature. Whatever his area of interest, he's more likely to be a traditionalist than a pioneer. If the Shih Tzu is a therapist, he's the kind who listens quietly, occasionally offering a calm, "So, how do you feel about that?" If you want someone to tell you how to fix your life, see Dr. Phil.

Best Match with: Career women, women who enjoy being pampered
Bad Breed for: Tractor pull enthusiasts, rough sex advocates

SILKY TERRIER

He has the smarts, the will, and the energy to make his way in the world, but isn't one of those bossy men who will try and push you around. Though he enjoys having his way, he employs playful nudging rather than sledgehammer tactics. His sense of humor will get him through many doors that might otherwise be closed to him. The King of Schmooze, the Silky loves to network. He turns on the charm where a lesser man would turn up the pressure. Socially, the Silky is a dream. His high-spirited and joyful demeanor attracts business and friendships. While he's friendly, he isn't indiscriminate. Unlike men in the Sporting Dog group, he isn't likely to drag home psychotics and strays. Affectionate and responsive, he's never needy. He's a loving guy who doesn't smother you with love.

Heart: The Silky man is tougher and more vigorous than most Companion Dogs. He'll never start a fight, but if he feels threatened, he'll go at it with everything he's got. An understanding companion will gently remind him to pick his battles carefully. Otherwise, your Silky man might become scattered. So many wrongs to right, so little time.

Head: His perfectionism can suck the joy out of any task and your Silky may rage at himself, or curse under his breath while he's working. Don't let it upset you. It isn't directed toward you. Anger can motivate and, as long as he's crabbing, he isn't depressed. He appreciates humor, so try joking him out of his bad mood.

> The great thing about a Silky? No matter how bad things get, you won't find him moaning into his beer.

Family: While the Silky makes a better father than many in the Companion Group, he isn't exactly a natural in the Dad department. If he gets too busy, he may neglect his relationship with the kids. Draw his attention to the problem and he'll try to make it right. If he had only realized! You may want to set up regular family meetings, or insist that he make it home for a sit-down dinner. If you want him to make it to Junior's soccer game, stash a loving reminder in his briefcase.

Work: He's a man who doesn't miss deadlines. While having similar interests to those of the Chihuahua, the Silky's approach to his work is "soft sell" in comparison to his yappy pal. Like his namesake dog, bred to kill rats and snakes, the Silky Man is drawn to jobs that let him "exterminate vermin." He may be an investigative journalist, or an attorney working in areas like consumer protection or environmental law. You may find him patrolling the Internet, tracking perpetrators of cyber-crime.

Best Match with: Funny, positive women.
Bad Breed for: Nervous Nellies, worrywarts.

YORKSHIRE TERRIER

There are a few things you will need to invest in once you're involved with a Yorkie man. First, invest in a good multi-vitamin. If you're not in top physical form, this man will wear you out. If you can't keep up with him, he may leave you behind. Second, invest in yoga classes or some type of meditation. If you're not centered, you'll go nuts trying to figure out how and why this man reacts the way he does. He's unpredictable, emotionally unstable, stubborn, and quite willful. Interesting? Yes. Easy? Never. Finally, invest in a good shrink... one who won't tire of hearing you say, "I love him, but I want to kill him!" If you can't afford a shrink, try a twelve-step program. Any twelve-step program. Adult partners of adult children might do the trick.

Heart: A permanent two-year-old, the Yorkie's favorite song is "I Won't Grow Up." On the one hand, jolly and spunky, on the other suspicious and manipulative, this man can be quite a handful. He'll try almost anything to get his way. Like a selfish toddler, you can almost hear him screaming, "Mine! Mine! Mine!" When he isn't screaming, he'll be looking up at you with those big, sad eyes, as though to say, "You know you want to forgive me!"

Head: Territorial to the Nth degree, the Yorkshire man likes to run the show and will take on much bigger men, both in the office and in the local pub. Like the youthful Peter Pan fencing with Captain Hook, he'll dance circles around an opponent, dazzling onlookers with verbal thrusts and parries.

Family: The Yorkie makes an unreliable and inconsistent parent and the pressures of parenthood can feel overwhelming to him. The noise and constant motion get on his nerves. He snaps at the children. He may enter their rooms and rifle through their belongings, looking for evidence of a crime. He can sometimes favor one child over another, even going so far as to intercede in arguments to take the favored child's side.

Work: The Yorkie is no office wallflower. Love him or hate him, you're sure to know who he is. He understands office politics and never underestimates his own appeal. A Yorkie man can "suck up" with the best of 'em. Your best chance of beating him at the office game is to make sure one of his catty remarks at the water cooler is overheard by the boss. If he is your boss, he's either in your face, or looking over your shoulder.

Best Match with: Patient but firm partners.
Bad Breed for: Pushovers.

Head 'em Up, Move 'em Out
The Herding Breeds

HERDING DOG MEN

Herding Dogs were bred for instinct and decision making ability and Herding Dog Men are independent thinkers. Overachievers, workaholics, obsessives and control freaks, these men need to work and to organize. Bold and brave, they are leaders, not followers.

In the dating stage, a Herder can be infuriating. After your first romantic night together, he gets wrapped up with work and forgets to call. If you're a woman who likes to linger over coffee and dessert, this is not the man for you. He's got the check before you've put the fork in your Flounder Florentine. Suggest taking an afternoon nap and your Herding Dog will look at you like you're the one from Mars!

Though he's a power in the work place, your Herder won't be into the "Two Martini Lunch." He prefers to order in a sandwich so that he can update the filing system during his break. He may irritate co-workers by calling an impromptu meeting, just when everyone else is preparing to leave for the day. Herders love sending out memos.

Unlike the Terriers, men in the Herding Dog group have the ability to convince others to help them build an empire or achieve their vision. If you're not careful, your Herding Dog Man will try herding you. In this case, distracting him with outside work is a better strategy than simply refusing to budge. If your Herder doesn't have a corporation to run, try signing him up as a soccer coach. In fact, herding dogs can make great dads for large families. You'll see them driving vanloads of kids to school events, or organizing sack races and tug-o-war at the Boy Scout Camporee. They are politicians, Little League coaches,

CEO's of large corporations, contractors, producer/directors and evangelists. Whatever they do, they'll try to convince others to come along for the ride. Steven Spielberg and Bill Gates came to mind for me.

AUSTRALIAN CATTLE DOG
(Queensland Heeler or Blue Heeler)

Like the scrappy-but-battered boxing champ who won't throw in the towel, the Australian Cattle Dog man doesn't know the meaning of the word quit. Heelers are rough and rugged and enjoy hurling themselves into physical activity. You might find him playing in a local rugby game. If he gets hurt, even if he's hurt badly, you'll never get him to the hospital before the game is over. "Naw, man, I'm okay," he'll protest, as blood pours from the three-inch gash in his forehead, "Lemme back in the game!" The Heeler gives new meaning to the term "workaholic." Work is work. Play is work. Love is work. Kids are work. Sex is work. Fun is work. This man does not relax. People who don't get him think he's inconsiderate. Mid-conversation, he'll interrupt you to leave a message for a co-worker. He'll walk out of your daughter's dance recital because he remembers something he left at the office. And, yes, he will answer the phone while you're having sex.

Heart: The Heeler man will not be fun on vacation, unless your idea of fun is hitting every point of interest in the vacation guide on the first day, then moving on to the next city. This guy does not consider relaxation an achievement. A tip… If you're desperate for a vacation, take him on a cruise. There are no phones and no way off the ship. Just make sure you accidentally leave the laptop at home.

Head: He enjoys anything he perceives as a challenge. If something's not challenging, he'll make it that way. A date for drinks at your favorite bar can become a contest, if he sees another man look your way. He'll confront the would-be suitor with a menacing, "What're you lookin' at?" Lucky for you (and him) he's got a really good macho bluff. Ninety-nine percent of the time, even his more formidable adversaries back down.

Family: Terrific with go-along kids, a Heeler dad can be non-stop fun. His kids will have souvenirs from every theme park and season tickets to every home game. But strong-willed, independent kids may think they were spawned by Satan. If this is the case at your house, it's best to step in and take over the bulk of the parental responsibilities.

If you really want to help your Heeler, help him learn to prioritize. He attacks every task as though it were of ultimate importance and could benefit from the knowledge that some things can be delegated, left for later, or not done at all.

Work: Heelers make excellent project managers, when they can say, "These are my ten people and this is my goal." He might be a theatrical agent in Hollywood or a minor league baseball manager in Des Moines. You won't find him in a home office doing solitary work. He needs hustle and bustle and will be at his best with people working under him.

Best Match with: Partners who can hold their own.
Bad Breed for: Co-dependents, the overly sensitive.

AUSTRALIAN SHEPHERD

Most of us remember the old nursery rhyme, about the little girl with the wayward curl and the incredible mood swings:

"There was a little girl who had a little curl,
Right in the middle of her forehead.
When she was good she was very, very good,
But when she was bad she was horrid."

That little girl must share a few genes with our Australian Shepherd man. Fast-moving and quick-thinking, he's beautiful, brilliant, energetic, hard-working, and dotes on you as if you were royalty. Or... he's neurotic, insecure, overly protective and testy. These are the two sides of the Aussie coin.

Heart: Which side of his coin comes up depends a lot on you. If you can help him channel his energy he will be the best of partners. Unlike the Heeler man, an Aussie can relax and have fun. As with the Heeler, you'll pack a lot into a short vacation, but you won't feel like you're being dragged through the museum with a stopwatch ticking loudly.

Head: Plan ahead for his retirement. An Aussie without a busy schedule is not a happy camper. He doesn't need a hobby. He needs a mission. If he doesn't have a mission, you will become his mission. And if you think you need more space now, just wait. The golden years won't seem so golden with him buried in your side like a big fat tick.

Family: He's great with kids, but he will tend to treat them like a herd. You'll often find him at the wheel of a minivan filled to bursting with a pint-sized soccer team. He's almost certain to be the team coach. You might occasionally need to intercede on your kids' behalf, suggesting that youngsters need free time for unstructured play.

Work: You'll find him in jobs requiring great attention to detail. He's able to process large amounts of information and quickly make decisions based in that information. Air traffic control might appeal to him, or mutual fund management. High-tech, fast-moving businesses attract him. If he's your boss, you'd do well to remember that he's always watching. He may implement drug testing in the office.

Best Match with: Creative, go-getter types.
Bad Breed for: Boring or sedentary partners.

BELGIAN
(Belgian Malinois, Belgian Sheepdog, Belgian Tervuren)

An incredible combination of brains and brawn, the Belgian man is unquestionably masculine and his physical prowess is matched only by his intellectual capacity. This is a man that all women want and few are suited to live with. He can be quite a handful for the wrong woman. A Belgian man needs the chase, so those who desire a predictable ride should steer clear. He's bored by predictability and your life will be turned upside-down if he feels that you're reining him in. Though he's not standoffish, Mr. Belgian will scrutinize anyone who enters his domain. Some see him as aloof, others say he's cautious and, occasionally, he'll run people off with his manly presence. A cross-armed Belgian at the door is enough to keep a nosy neighbor from barging into your house for a peek. If you are an extremely social person who invites anyone and everyone into your life, you might want to plan your get-togethers for a time when he's at work.

Head: Because he trusts his instincts, he'll never be a by-the-book guy. Though he's dedicated to his job, he'll break rank if he feels his idea or hunch is the right one.

Heart: He keeps his distance with strangers, but is just the opposite with the ones he loves. You'll be hard-pressed to find private time once you've chosen a Belgian mate. Have a lock installed on your bathroom door unless you're a big believer in two's company. Still, he's not touchy-feelie, he's more the strong silent type. He won't want to analyze the details of your relationship. He just wants to be with you.

> If your child or teenager is a Belgian, watch who he's running with. A trouble-making friend can easily influence him. Once he's matured, this usually isn't a problem

Family: Belgian's are loving and protective dads. While he believes his own kids may have hung the moon, he'll be far less forgiving of other folks' offspring. He's not at his best with nervous or high-strung kids, as he's affected by their energy and noise level. Your normally devoted dad could become snappy and irritable.

Work: A Belgian excels in work that offers a fresh challenge every day. If he's in law enforcement, he's smart enough to figure out where the "perp" is hiding and tough enough to bring him down. The Belgian's love for the chase might mean a career in medical research, or he may be a day trader, chasing profits on the Internet. If he's a lawyer, he's probably a lawyer with a cause. He has the look of someone who will never back down.

Best Match with: The one-man women, tough love advocates. **Bad Breed for**: Nervous Nellies, status quo babes, the confrontation-shy.

BORDER COLLIE

If this man reads a book he likes, he'll pick up every other title by that author and that will be the only topic of conversation until he's done with all of them. If he hears a funny "scritch" coming from his engine, you may wake in the middle of the night to find him in the garage, completely surrounded by dismantled car. On Friday he rents the movie "Braveheart," by Monday the house is filled with Scottish music CDs, then he's taking bagpiping lessons, and before you know it, you're living in Glasgow and learning to like Haggis. Let's hope Victoria's Secret has a line of thong undies in Royal Stuart tartan, because that's the only way you'll get his attention while he's in this phase. This guy's obsessive. He's compulsive. He's our Border Collie man.

Heart: It's crazy love! Every date is an adventure. His friends say he's obsessed with you. He's interested in the whole world, dives head-long into life, and wants to take you along for the ride. You're head over heels, dizzy with desire. Then... he moves in. Can you say "high maintenance?"

Warning! When the relationship's over, every other man you meet will seem dull and gray compared to him.

Head: Never expect to win an argument with a Border Collie mate. He's too smart, too perceptive, incredibly persistent, and he never gets tired of arguing.

Family: He'll expect his kids to be passionate about his passions and he's passionate about everything. He'll sign them up for soccer one week, chess club the next, dramatics the week after that. And he'll expect them to do everything they do REALLY well. If he fails at breaking their young spirits, expect violent battles during the teen years.

Work: Anything that becomes his obsession can become his work. He's the entrepreneur who creates a string of successful companies, sells each for a bundle once it's up and running, to move on to his next obsession. Just as likely, he finds himself unable to let go of a failed business and, determined to drag it into the red at any cost, may lose everything.

Best Match with: Adrenaline junkies, or those loose enough to enjoy a wild ride.
Bad Breed for: The uptight, quick-tempered chicks, Martha Stewart wannabes.

BOUVIER DES FLANDRES

Like Popeye the sailor, the Bouvier might say, "I yam what I yam." During adolescence, that sudden surge of testosterone becomes rocket fuel in the teenaged Bouv. He's the young guy in the hot car, cutting dangerously in and out of traffic on the Thruway. Under his high school yearbook photo, you see he's been voted "most likely to end up in a bar brawl." No, he's not a vicious sociopath. He's just full of manly energy and doesn't know what to do with it. He'll calm down as he gets older. At least, you'll never have to worry about the Bouvier getting into trouble with his buddies. He doesn't have pack mentality. You won't lose him to the company softball team or to the neighborhood bowling league. It's not that he's anti-social, he just plain doesn't care much about outside people.

Head: A Bouvier man looks at other humans as though they were filling a spot he's overqualified for. He's smart, his kids are smart, his wife is smart, and everyone else is bringing down the curve.

Heart: When everything's going well, the Bouv is a real sweetheart. But at the first sign of impending danger, he's commanding the troops and circling the wagons. He's a shoot first, ask questions later guy. A cool-headed woman will need to step in, from time to time, to temper her blustering Bouv.

Family: As much as he loves you, be prepared to play second fiddle to his kids. He's a true believer in the old adage, "Blood is thicker than water." So, don't make disparaging remarks about his mother, or comment that his brother is a ne'er-do-well. His loyalty will blind him to his family's faults. Try reverse psychology. Make excuses for the judgmental old bat and point out that most cheating, gambling, alcoholic wife-beaters are really just misunderstood victims of a changing society. He might kick the brother out of the basement and tell the old woman to butt out of his personal life. Maybe.

Work: Bright, observant, and decisive, the Bouv is a natural as a paramedic. He'd be great at flying Coast Guard rescue missions, though other military careers would not work for this man. He's too much of an original thinker. He's self-motivated and could certainly run a business, but he'd be better off in a family business or a one-man operation.

Best Match with: Bright, even-tempered women, therapists, and saints.
Bad Breed for: Martyrs, insecure women, needies.

BRIARD

For those of you who saw the movie Saving Private Ryan, our Briard would've been the stalwart Jimmy Ryan, ready to disobey an order to remain with his buddies on the front. The Briard Man has spirit and initiative. He's fearless, with no trace of timidity. The four-footed Briard was bred for duty in war, carrying messages to the front line, searching for wounded soldiers, pulling carts and patrolling. Likewise, our Briard man might find his career in some branch of the military, the Marines being his most likely choice. The Briard is a work hard, play hard, high-energy man. Very territorial, you will never fret about prowlers with this man on guard. He's not a naturally tolerant soul. Left to his own devices, a Briard would never leave his neighborhood. You can help him expand his horizons by taking him out of his element and introducing him to a variety of different people. Show him that not everyone outside his own herd is a predator.

Head: Though he's not a deep thinker, he has a straightforward, intuitive intelligence. He understands that, in many situations, it is possible to think too much.

Heart: To have a happy life with a Briard, you'll need to keep things interesting. If your first two dates were dinner and a movie, try showing up for the third date on a motorcycle, dressed like Ann-Margaret in "Kitten with a Whip." If you're married to him (as you may well be after the Ann-Margaret stunt), you'll need to be creative. Mix things up. Never give him a list of daily chores. He'll take the trash out for a couple of weeks, then snap and heave the Hefty bag out the upstairs window.

Family: He's a protective, vigilant father who really wants to be involved with his kids. With a Briard heading your household, the warning "Wait until your father gets home" really packs a punch. Discipline problems won't be tolerated and teamwork will be his mantra. On any given day you might hear, "We're all picking up our rooms now!" or "Everybody in the car, pronto!" or "If Timmy doesn't finish his homework, nobody gets to go!" Counter his pushiness with gentle persuasion and a loving spirit.

> Briards do not forgive and forget. He'll remember every unkind word and critical remark and will carry the resentment like a smelly old dufflebag filled with dirty laundry. When an argument starts, the entire contents of that bag may be thrown in your face.

Work: A Briard likes physical work. He's more likely to be a beat cop than a detective. If he plays pro football, he'll probably be a running back, protecting the ball and weaving through his opponents by sheer instinct. If you own a bar, you'll want a Briard as your bouncer. He doesn't need to use force to get rid of people. He wills them out the door. A Briard dislikes repetition, so a job on the line at the widget factory will not work for him.

Best Match with: Tolerant, charitable, social partners.
Bad Breed for: Eggheads, critics, hot house flowers.

COLLIE

Go out with a Collie man and you may find yourself saying, "This guy is too good to be true!" And guess what? You may be right. Okay, okay... he is ruggedly handsome. He's friendly and outgoing… the kind of guy who will warmly hug everyone you introduce him to. And yes, he is responsible. Trustworthy and dependable, he's the guy who'll show up to help you move. He'll help everybody move. He'll use his own truck to move you. Your Mom beams with pride when you bring him to the family reunion. Even your Dad is impressed with him. He probably played high school or even college sports… no individual athletic heroics, though. The Collie is a team player, not the star quarterback. That trophy in his den more than likely reads: "All-State Honorable Mention Corner Back." So if you need to bask in the light of a star, walk right on by the Collie!

Head: The Collie man is bright and will probably have a degree… a practical degree, in a field like business or engineering. He is not a highly original thinker. He's not going to invent that new computer chip that revolutionizes the electronics industry.

Heart: He'd rather be home with you than out at a strip club, buying drinks for clients. He won't fight those five guys at the neighborhood bar, defending your honor. He's more likely to try and joke them out of their fighting mood while you slip out the back door. So, if you need Trump, Bronson, and Einstein rolled into one, this is not the man for you.

> **It's a fact... He'll be miserable with a woman who criticizes him. He won't fight with you. He'll just leave.**

Family: He's the best of dads and will bend over backwards to please you and the kids. But, please keep your expectations in check. He's not superman, he's just plain super.

Work: Collie men are hard workers. He won't take sick days and he won't run off when he turns forty because he's just discovered his life has no meaning. His life does have meaning. Even if he works in a ball-bearing plant, he'll find meaning in it.

Best Match with: The more traditional woman.
Bad Breed for: Eccentrics or academics, critical women.

GERMAN SHEPHERD

Are you the kind of gal who is consistently drawn to Rottweiler men, often with disastrous results? Please stop, breathe deeply, and take a moment to consider the German Shepherd man. If he hears that prowler on the front porch, this guy will call 911 first. Then he'll move you and the kids to a safe room in the back of the house. Then he'll stand guard at the door. And if the cops don't show up? No problem. He can back up his bark with his bite. If the German Shepherd man is a cop, he's the proverbial Good Cop. Don't get me wrong, he's no pushover. You will have to lay down the law once in awhile

Head: The good news is that German Shepherd men are smart enough to listen and adaptable enough to change. Okay, okay... he won't talk to you about his "inner child," but he will let you know when he's had a bad day.

Heart: Finding out how he feels about his bad day may take some work. He doesn't want to appear weak and he doesn't want to burden you with problems he should be able to handle himself. Remind him that you're tough too and he'll eventually learn to trust you with his feelings.

> A Tip ...
> Give him a good reason for anything you want to do. If you bark orders at him, he becomes as stubborn as a mule.

Family: He's great with children and, unlike other dominant breeds, is not overly bossy with his family. He tends to be cooperative, solving problems in weekly family meetings. He'll insist that the kids sit down at the table for dinner, but that's because he wants to hear about their day, not because he wants to rule the family with an iron fist.

Work: Highly intelligent and quite adaptable, numerous fields are open to the GS man. He reads people well, but probably won't be a therapist. That's a little too touchy-feelie for him. He may be a corporate headhunter, police detective, parole officer, criminal profiler, or juvenile caseworker. He may also do well in search and rescue work.

Best Match with: Diplomatic, cooperative women.
Bad Breed for: Strident, bossy women.

OLD ENGLISH SHEEP DOG

May I suggest, as I did with the Rottweiler, that you meet the mother? With the Old English man, you can get a big, sweet, cuddly, teddy bear... or you can get a big, blustering, domineering windbag with the IQ of a peach pit. But hey, let's give him the benefit of the doubt. You've met his family and they're right out of a Norman Rockwell painting. Great! Now we can tell you about the wonderful man you're falling for. The Old English man is a social butterfly. He'll enjoy New Years Eve at Times Square just as much as an intimate dinner party. He'll be a caring, fun-loving and watchful dad. Your home will be a meeting place for friends and family. The cookouts will always be in your backyard, as will all the neighborhood kids. And don't worry about your sexy, single neighbor, Suzanne. He won't be looking for greener pastures, and he won't cheat on you. A lovable jokester, he's the guy everyone gathers around at the office water cooler. Your kids will adore him, though he might be too permissive with them. Like others in this group, he'll always be willing to gather them up and herd them around.

Head: Old English men can be very hardheaded. If you become an irresistible force, he'll be glad to play the immovable object. While he's not an intellectual, he is a problem solver and the family diplomat. He doesn't reason out solutions, he feels them out.

Heart: He really loves his home, so you might have to remind your Old English that getting away for the weekend is a good idea. Unless you're a convincing debater, be prepared to work around his schedule. The Rock of Gibraltar he's not. You'll have to get used to his moody days. Then again, sometimes unpredictable is interesting.

Family: Old English men are not at their best when they are overly tired or stressed. They can quickly become irritated with kids who aren't going along. That's when you need to herd him… away from the kids and onto the couch for a nap. Be careful, though. He's not a self-starter and may spend more time on the couch than in the gym. Try joining him for a brisk walk in the morning. He'll be more energetic if you encourage him to exercise and help him watch his weight.

Work: Not great at taking orders, an Old English man does better as an employer than as an employee. He's at his best when he's running the show. When he's working with a team, his teammates almost always defer to him. Old English social skills are legendary. He'll shine in careers that let him use his charm and humor to advantage. He may be a motivational speaker.

You may find him in local politics. He might be an executive at an ad agency. Old English taxi drivers make huge tips.

Best Match with: Perceptive, easy-going partners, cheerleaders.
Bad Breed for: "My way or the highway" types, crowd haters

PULI

You've seen him bouncing down the street... the guy who exudes an air of masculine self-confidence... the one that seems to spring as he walks, arms swinging, head turning, and always with a big "I am it on a stick" smile plastered on his face. You find yourself drawn to him. Who is he? What makes him so self-assured? Is he really all that? Or is he just another puffed up, macho, unemployed, unattached windbag? The answer to all your questions is quite simple. This man is a Puli... a true combination of it-on-a-stick and puffed-up windbag. You say you've got to have him? Then make sure you don't appear too eager. If you don't make yourself stand out from the crowd, a Puli man will treat you like just another sheep in his flock. Play hard to get, or you may find yourself just tagging along with him. You'll be going to his movie, eating at his restaurant, wearing the clothes he picks out for you, waiting for him to call you for a date.

Head: Arguments will not be fun. Puli men are exceedingly smart and, if he can't figure out how to win fairly, he'll figure out another way to win. Or he'll put his fist through the wall. He's used to getting his way, so on those rare occasions when he doesn't, watch out! Pulis can be sore losers. He won't beat you up, but he'll beat something up. The same energy that makes him so appealing when things are going his way, can make him seem awfully unstable when the tables are turned.

Heart: Pulis don't really care if other people like them. Why should he care? After all, he likes him and he's the best person he knows. He actually says things like, "God, I'm good!"... or, "Enough about me, what do you think about me?"...or, "I can't wait till tomorrow, cause I get better looking every day!" And he means it.

Family: Forget about hyphenating your kid's last name. A Puli man wants his name, and only his name, on everything that's his. (You will frequently find yourself having the "you don't own me" conversation.) He'll be a good provider but, as with a lot of these herding men, God help the child who doesn't want to go along. He'll be a lot easier on his girls than his boys.

Work: Thanks to his high intelligence, a Puli man will be successful in whatever field he chooses. Don't look for him in manual labor jobs or fields that require people skills. This man runs the company and all the people in the company. He's smart enough to hire a people person to work under him, so that his employees don't quit right away.

Best Match with: Supremely confident, push back types
Bad Breed for: Shrinking violets, low self-esteem gals

SHETLAND SHEEPDOG

The Sheltie man is for the woman who likes her Herders with less brawn and more brain. He's much less of a macho man than his steadfast herding cousins. Because he's so intensely loving and devoted, it would never occur to a Sheltie that you might be having an affair. In fact, you'll have to go out of your way to make him jealous. It's not that he's taking you for granted. He's just really, really trusting. Don't play the jealousy game with him. He won't get it. He's highly sensitive and it will devastate him if he thinks you're really fooling around on him. One problem you might have is that this man is so comfortable with you, he might lose his friends. Make sure you keep getting him out and around other people. There's no such thing as too much togetherness for this guy. You, on the other hand… ?

Heart: Shelties are exceedingly giving partners. A real "what's mine is yours" man. He's adaptable and cooperative, preferring to solve problems diplomatically, rather than with his fists. The Sheltie can take care of himself, so he doesn't mind giving you as much space as you need. He's a great match for a career-centered woman.

Head: He tends to be a worrier and, depending on the individual, may be quite neurotic. But he's just worried about your future. Will there be enough money in the bank to fund your retirement? Might that minor problem at work mushroom into something he can't handle? All the worrying may make him irritable, so that he snaps at you. He never means it. Once you call it to his attention, he's all over himself trying to make it right.

Family: He's not the life of the party, preferring family and work to chitchat with strangers. When his family life is calm and stable, his mind is free to be productive. The Sheltie man is loyal and very devoted. He's usually good with children, though you may have to remind him to be positive with them.

Work: This man is a thinker, but uses his intellect in practical ways. He probably won't be an artist or philosopher. He's the guy who invents the new computer chip, or discovers a cure for that disease. His ability to listen (and perhaps the need to understand his own phobias) may lead him to a career in psychiatry. If you're his boss, know that an aggressive management style will turn the Sheltie into your enemy. If you're his employee, understand that his constant fretting has nothing to do with your job performance.

Best Match with: Intelligent, independent, trustworthy partners.
Bad Breed for: Worrywarts, nags, teases, users

WELSH CORGI

You want to invite Jack and Mary to your party. Your Corgi likes Mary, but can't stand Jack, and will never understand why you have to invite both of them, even though they're engaged. You insist on inviting them, the result being that you're tense the whole evening, worrying about what he might be saying to Jack and wondering why Mary's crying in the corner. A good relationship with a Corgi man takes some work. He's pushy and you'll have to learn to push back. If he asks what restaurant you'd like to dine in, name a restaurant, or forever hold your peace. Once you've uttered the phrase, "I don't know, where do you want to go?" he may never ask again. He'll just take you to his favorite.

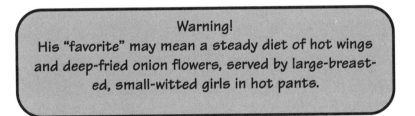

Warning!
His "favorite" may mean a steady diet of hot wings and deep-fried onion flowers, served by large-breasted, small-witted girls in hot pants.

Heart: He'll only run over you if you let him. A woman with chutzpah can even the playing field quickly. Passive women, whiners and couch potatoes make him miserable.

Head: He really enjoys a lively debate. Just make sure you have the goods to back up your point, or you'll find yourself talking to the back of his head. Convince him and he's one of the few men who will happily concede that you're right.

Family: He's great with kids, but won't allow them to be lazy. Life's too short to waste a day lounging in front of a South Park marathon. He'll also make snap judgments about their friends and will quickly weed out any he feels are "bad seeds". If a subtle "keep away" suggestion won't work, he'll just pick up and move to a new school district.

Work: Corgi men are good at organizing and sorting out problems... separating the wheat from the chaff. You might find him in charge of triage in an Emergency Room, deciding whose problem needs attention first. He may be the company's personnel manager, deciding who is hired or fired. He may be a high-priced consultant, brought in to help decide which departments need beefing up, and which need to be cut.

Best Match with: Self-possessed, career-minded women.
Bad Breed for: Amateur therapists and Little Black Rainclouds.

Princes and Paupers
The Non-Sporting Breeds

NON-SPORTING DOGS

The one thing most Non-Sporting Dog Men have in common is that work is not their first priority. In the most extreme cases, there is absolutely no use for whatever it is they know how to do. In others, they are employable, but something less than driven. These men range from members of royalty to that guy with the tin cup on the subway. From the dashing Dalmatian to the cranky Chinese Chow Chow to the bulky Bulldog, there's a Non-Sporting Dog breed for every woman who doesn't need a workhorse.

The Non-Sporting Man is sometimes independently wealthy (usually from an inheritance), or he's a sweet-talking con man, charming his way through life. Some Non-Sporting breeds make good escorts at high society galas. Others are couch potatoes, a last resort for women who just simply can't live without a ring on their finger. Still others are philosophers, dreamers, or easily bored men who jump from job to job. Any member of any royal family falls into this group, as does the boss's nephew, polo players, country club tennis pros, male models, gigolos, nobility, welfare recipients, and big, sweet slugs. In their favor is the fact that most Non-Sporting Men are adorable and easy to live with. If you care less about money than love, you may well find your match in this group.

BICHON FRISE

Dear Dog Lady,

I am hopelessly attracted to intelligent and/or eccentric men and have spent my best years ping-ponging back and forth between self-centered Sight Hounds and control freak Herders. How can I break this vicious cycle?

Exhausted in Boston

Dear Exhausted,

Have I got a man for you! As interesting as a Sight Hound and as smart as a Herder, the Bichon Frise is even-keeled and cheerful. Extremely sociable, he loves you, loves kids, loves strangers and often drags them home. Still, he's not likely to be taken advantage of. Unlike his friendly cousins in the Sporting Dog Group, he'll smell the con artist before he's able to settle in for the night. A Bichon man won't try to boss you and is always willing to talk things through. He's never demanding, is quite cooperative, and he makes a wonderful life partner. (There's a big BUT coming here…) He cannot be left alone for long periods of time. He gets crazy when he's left alone. Be careful. Your women friends will love this guy. Women who aren't your friends will love him, too. Though he isn't usually inclined to roam, BEWARE! A very determined female may carry him off.

Heart: If you hurt him, he'll withdraw from you and you'll have quite a time regaining his trust. If you hurt him repeatedly, he'll retaliate.

Head: He's dependable and emotionally stable, but not so much so that he becomes boring. (No one this smart could ever be boring!) This man is not afraid of change.

Family: He's very active indoors and that's where he's likely to work and play. He doesn't care much for anything outdoors and is definitely not a camper. If you want an Eagle Scout, look elsewhere, and if your family needs protection, hire a body-guard. He can be a pushover... especially with the kids. "Sure you can have that coke before bed!"

Work: Your Bichon will never step on others to try and get ahead. He doesn't need to. People will love him and they will give him work. He'll be able to function in any arena where a combination of smarts, charm, and energy are necessary, but he'll never be CEO of a major corporation. Don't send him in to negotiate, unless you need someone to play Good Cop to another man's Bad. If he's a teacher, he's the teacher all the students love.

Best Match with: Intelligent, social, attentive partners.
Bad Breed for: Crocodile hunters, tough broads, absent partners, gold diggers.

BOSTON TERRIER

Ask and ye shall receive. That's the motto of the Boston man. The last bite of his dessert? No problem. Feel like drinking his last beer? Go for it! The Boston Man is giving, trusting, gentle, easy to live with, and is rarely an irritating housemate. You may even forget he's there. Still, he can be rather emotional. When he's happy, the world is filled with sunshine and laughter. When he's down, it's as though the "Veil of Mordor" has descended over his realm. Since he never blames you for his woes, or tries to drag you down with him, this just serves to make him an interesting companion. The Boston has lots of energy in his youth, but will want a quieter life as he ages.

Heart: This man won't be happy with a gloomy, pessimistic woman, as your dark moods will depress him. Likewise, your thoughtful acts and warm I-love-you's will help to keep him smiling.

Head: He doesn't think well when he's upset, so any problem you have at home will cause him problems at the office. Though he usually gets along well with other men, a pushy, aggressive male may irritate him and cause him to push back. If forced to work with a pushy guy, he won't be able to stand it and will have to find another job.

Family: Devoted and caring, he makes an excellent father, but will enjoy reading a bedtime story more than roughhousing with the kids.

Work: Bright and cooperative, he's a great co-worker. He's not shy about offering his ideas, yet not overly attached to them. He thinks your ideas are great, too! He's more likely to be found in middle management than in the corner office or out on the loading dock. Like others of this group, he has probably drifted into his occupation and doesn't have a true calling.

Best Match with: Positive, demonstrative partners.
Bad Breed for: Rough handlers, women who love to argue.

BULLDOG

An old family friend, known affectionately as Aunt Thelma, grew up in a large family of ten children. Eight of them were girls. Of the eight girls, seven married early in life and one, Aunt Thelma, stayed a spinster until her late thirties. Determined not to be the only unmarried sister in the family, Aunt Thelma met and married Uncle Rupert just before her fortieth birthday. Rupert was a forty-five year old bachelor who lived with his elderly mother, sold farm equipment for a living, and always looked like he was having a bad day. Uncle Rupert was a Bulldog. In short, the Bulldog is the man for any woman who simply wants to be able to say, "This is my husband." On the plus side, you will never be lonely. He will be your constant companion, as he has almost no interest in anything that doesn't include a big comfy chair and a TV remote. He won't be out with the boys, he won't take off for fishing weekends, and he'll never cheat on you. He just doesn't have the energy. He will also enjoy your cooking. He'll have to, since he will never cook.

Heart: The Bulldog is a simple soul. He wheezes, snores, drools, and passes gas as nonchalantly as most people pass the salt. It would never occur to him that this behavior might be considered rude. Sleeping and eating are his only hobbies. But look on the bright side... he's easy to please. If you remember to pick up his beer, put some food in front of him and remember to pay the cable bill, you'll rarely hear a peep out of him.

Head: A Bulldog man gives the phrase "stuck in his ways" a whole new meaning. If he doesn't want to do it, you'll never be able to force him. The more you push, the more he hunkers down. He is so predictable you can set your watch by his beer-drinking ritual.

It takes extreme provocation to get this man upset, but once aroused, he can be dangerous. Still, he's not likely to be dangerous with you. The most upset you'll ever see him is if you misplace his TV Guide. Any problems he may have are with other men.

Family: He loves you and the kids, likes spending time with you, and your family will feel safe with a Bulldog Dad in the house. God, help the intruder who ventures into a Bulldog's home! He's not the guy who pummels a burglar to death with his fistsg. He's the guy who keeps a semi-automatic in the closet. He's going for the ultimate amount of destruction for the least amount of physical energy expended. Don't wake him in the night unless you're sure that noise in the garage isn't your neighbor Sam sneaking in to retrieve his Craftsman ratchet set.

Work: He might be a trucker or he might work on an assembly line. He will not be self-employed, unless you run the business and he does the legwork. He can't deal with a boss looking over his shoulder. That brings out his stubborn streak.

Best Match with: Lonely spinsters, the very easily pleased.
Bad Breed for: Active or uptight women, prudes, artists, or intellectuals.

CHOW CHOW

He's regal, aloof, and extremely independent, but there will be rules in a Chow Chow's house. These are the three commandments, according to the Chow Chow man: Thou shalt not push me, Thou shalt not yak at me, Thou shalt not mess with my stuff. This guy is bossy and very territorial. Not overly affectionate or demonstrative, he may experience your attempts to create closeness as "pawing" at him. Sex with a Chow man is not exactly a romantic adventure. It's more like the old joke about Irish foreplay... "Brace yourself Kathleen!" And no, he doesn't want to cuddle afterwards. He needs his own space and will protect his possessions like a mother lion protects her cubs. Unless you're a very strong soul, he'll appoint himself the family tyrant. A Chow man is extremely stubborn, controlling, and uncooperative, he has no sympathy for wimps. He finds weakness irritating and may snap at you if you appear indecisive or anxious. The best thing about him? He'll stick around, but won't bother you much.

Heart: If you allow this man to run the whole show, he certainly will, but he won't be completely happy about it. The Chow needs a partner he can respect, who will respect him in turn. If either half of this formula is missing, love can't last.

Head: Once he's set his mind to something, he's completely unwavering. He's not a blustery macho man. He won't yell. He'll just expect things to be done his way.

Family: If his family is loving and sociable, this will help to soften his hard edges. Still, he will never be a playful Dad. And don't expect him to change the dirty diaper or rock a screaming infant.

Work: While very intelligent, this man does not play well with others, and it can interfere with his ability to bring home the bacon. If you're his boss, you must understand that this is the man who wants your job. He's extremely independent and cannot be forced to do your will. If he's given a task that is absolutely under his control, he will excel. If he's the boss, he will not be able to delegate. If you work under him, prepare yourself for a hellish existence. He will hold you to his standards and they are ridiculously high.

Best Match with: Alpha females.
Bad Breed for: Hyperactive or emotionally needy women.

DALMATIAN

You've heard the phrase, "Jack of all trades, master of none?" That's our Dal man in a nutshell. He's a man who is all revved up with no place to go. His canine counterpart was once used as a coach dog, to follow and guard horse-drawn vehicles. The

202

carriage has since gone the way of rotary phone and, like the four-pawed version of the breed, Dalmatian men are workers in search of a job description. He can do a lot of things well, which can actually be a problem for a guy with the attention span of a gnat. Now, ask yourself, "Does he have good manners?" If he doesn't, you probably won't be able to teach him. Dals forget things. Where he put the keys. Where he parked the car. Where he was last night. He can also be a bit of a slob, leaving his things scattered around the house. Dals are accident prone, so he won't be a good match for a lady who collects porcelain figurines. On the plus side, he's cute and sweet and even trainable, if you have the patience of a saint and enough money to hire a maid.

Head: The Dalmatian's boundless but undirected energy can be annoying. His body follows his brain and his brain is always spinning off in new directions. He will follow you around the house, nosing into everything. A discipline like yoga, that combines meditation, breathing and physical activity, could help him learn to calm down… if you can convince him to try it.

Heart: He's willing to adapt to your needs, to the extent that his temperament will allow. Do not nag or wound this man, as it may well bring out a vicious streak.

Family: What about fatherhood? The rare Dal can rise to the occasion, provided he starts spending time with his offspring early in their infancy. But this man needs your attention and will not be happy in a home filled to bursting with children and strays... any kind of strays, the human or the animal varieties. Horses may be the exception to this rule and he may well love riding.

Work: The problem is in getting him to focus. Actually quite intelligent, the Dalmatian suffers from Attention Deficit Disorder. Physical, yet elegant, he's not for heavy lifting, but definitely needs a physical release for his tremendous energy. A job as country club tennis pro or ski instructor at a resort would be perfect for him. He might also make a good realtor. Though his books would be a mess, he'd love walking property lines with prospective buyers. If he's got "The Look," male model would be a good choice.

Best Match with: Good sports, exercise enthusiasts.
Bad Breed for: Short fuses, fragile egos, couch potatoes.

KEESHOND

You won't find this man in a singles' bar, so don't even try. Unlike many of his buddies, he's not out hunting for a one-night stand. You will have to go out and hunt for him. Keeshonds do not show off. If you don't get how great he is just by looking, he won't be interested in you either. Once you've found him, you'll be happy to know that you won't have to play games to keep his interest. Keeshond Men are concerned, first and foremost, with the relationship. He's not interested in the chase. If he can't read you, or feels you are not being honest, he will drop you like a pinless grenade. If you follow the "Rules" and wait three days to call him back, you will never hear from him again. He doesn't pursue pipe dreams, and is not likely to hit middle age and leave to find himself. Neither is he likely to run off after another woman

Heart: He's happy, affectionate, extroverted, and yes, energetic, but not annoyingly so. He'll find napping on the couch just as enjoyable as a party or family outing. A Keeshond loves a good time and good company. He gets along with men and women equally well.

Head: Okay, he's a little bit unpredictable, but not to the point of making you insane. He's cooperative, but not a pushover. You'll have to negotiate and learn to pick your battles with this man. Unless you're a sadist (or you're on the cabbage soup diet), this is not too much to ask.

Family: He'll love spending time with the kids and is playful and giving with them. When your teen dents his car or your toddler fills his new DVD player with squished grapes, he's the dad who'll say, "That's okay... they're just things."

Work: He's a man who stays put. He'll want to learn a job and do that job, which is not really a plus in a job market that rewards lifelong learning. Still, he does learn quickly when forced to learn. If he's older than 40,, he's not likely to have a job in the tech sector, though he may be among the digirati if he was raised with the technology. The Keeshond man is more comfortable working for others than having others work for him. He's a little too laid back to be self-employed.

Best Match with: Togetherness junkies, even-keel gals
Bad Breed for: Greta Garbo (recluses), ball-busters.

LHASA APSO

Just because he loves you, don't expect him to love your friends or even your family. A Lhasa man has five people he likes, two restaurants he enjoys and one neighborhood he'll live in. That is not going to change. While he's very extroverted (almost a show off!) with his inner circle, he's equally standoffish (or bor-derline rude) with strangers. Those who don't know him may think him arrogant or even a snob. The truth is, he's just plain suspicious of people he doesn't know and some he does know. At a small dinner party of very close friends, he will be incred-ibly charming, but a new acquaintance may be made to feel like a poor relation. Lhasa men can be bossy and domineering and if you're not up to the challenge, you're in for an unpleasant ride. He needs space for privacy. He'll share his things only if it's his idea. He needs things just so and may become upset when that isn't possible.

Heart: His problem with strangers may be connected to a deep-seated distrust of change. Once you've established a household, he will never want to move. Ever. And though he's smart enough to learn anything he needs to learn, he will not want to change jobs, unless he's forced to. The worst thing you can do to this man is to set off on a middle-aged quest to follow your bliss. He met you twenty years ago and doesn't want to suddenly find himself living with someone he doesn't recognize.

Head: Highly intelligent, the Lhasa man is also stubborn and strong-willed. Ask for one thing, he'll do the opposite. If you need him to do something for you, you must be both kind and firm. If you hurt or insult him, all is lost. Likewise, if he sees you as a wimp, he won't feel the need to oblige you.

Family: He's not great with kids. If you have older, very well-behaved children from a previous marriage, that will be fine. He will not enjoy the noise, mess, and roughhousing of young ones.

Work: He'll do fine in jobs that require a look of elegance and breeding. He'd make a great headwaiter at a pricey restaurant, where attitude is part of the job description. A career in the fashion industry would suit him well. Though he won't be a designer, he may be a buyer for an upscale store. If he has a job in the service industry, you can bet he'll be serving only the wealthiest people. If he's fortunate enough to be born into a royal family, he'll really be in his element. He'll love meeting heads of state, waving to his subjects, and sitting in the royal box at charity events.

Best Match with: Firm partners who are socially at ease.
Bad Breed for: Needies, pleasers, doormats and anyone with less-than-perfect taste.

POODLE

Forget the frou-frou image of the pampered little lap yap with the bad hairdo. This dog makes a great guy! One of the best. And he's tougher and more athletic than he looks. You may not notice the Poodle across that crowded room at the party, but when the guys take their shirts off for a dip in the pool... WOW! Temperament seems to be related to size with this breed. While all Poodle men are extroverted and highly intelligent, the big guys seem to be calmer and more social, while the smaller men are high-energy geniuses. If your Poodle man is king-sized, make sure he gets regular exercise. No matter what size package he comes in, a Poodle man is a sweetheart, a smart cookie and a great catch.

Heart: Affectionate, sensitive, and loving, he would never step on others, but neither will he allow himself to be stepped on. Your Poodle man will be very tuned into your feelings. He'll know instantly when something's wrong and you'll never have to tell him.

Head: As smart as they come. Really. No kidding. And smart without being nuts. Though he's a levelheaded fellow, he's never boring and is not adverse to change. He's the man who'd leave his job to move with you, if you were offered a better one.

Family: He's protective of his family but sensibly so, and will never make you feel like prisoners in your home. He'll want to drive his kids to school, rather than letting them get on the bus.

Work: This man is capable of achieving in almost any field he chooses. Amiable and cooperative, he's a joy to work with. The Poodle man is willing to take the helm when he's needed, but also works well with and for others. He's sure of himself but doesn't let his ego get in his way... or yours! If he has any problem making money, it will be because he has so many interests and is good at so many things. He may become bored with a job just about the time he starts bringing home the big bucks. If this happens, you'll have to make a decision. Do I want to live simply with a happy man or live high with a sad one?

Best Match with: Affectionate, self-assured partners.
Bad Breed for: Cold-shoulders.

SCHIPPERKE
(SKIP-er-kee)

The one thing you could never accuse him of is being wishy-washy. He loves it, he hates it, but he never, ever feels ambivalent about it. He's always ready for an adventure. While loyal and devoted to his family, the Schipperke man is quite independent. This independence makes his incredible energy level easier to live with. He will keep himself busy and won't need you to entertain him. Both mentally and physically agile, he never walks when he can run. The Schipperke is not the most social of men, but not because he dislikes people. He just has so much to do on his own that he can't be bothered with strangers. In one glance, he'll size a person up, decide if they'll ever be important to him, and forget about those who won't be. The Schipperke man can be quick-tempered, but the storm blows over as soon as it starts. You'll have to learn to walk away from arguments, as his opinion cannot be changed.

Heart: The Schipperke man has a great sense of humor and may be a practical joker. His close pals are crazy about him, though those outside the warmth of his immediate circle may not understand why. The worst wound this man could suffer is a wound to his pride.

Head: Extremely intelligent, his mind goes where his passion leads him, not necessarily where you want him to go. Hire someone else to repair your computer or tutor you in that new software. Oh, he could do it. But he keeps letting himself be distracted by other things... important things... his things.

> FYI...
> A locked door or a wrapped birth-day gift will drive him out of his mind. It will be opened!

Family: His family may be left on their own for long stretches of time. Be careful, though. If he's left alone for too long, this man can get squirrelly.

Work: Curiosity is the key. This man wants to know why things work and how. He may be a physicist, a philosopher, a theologian. Money is not terribly important to him and that may make problems for you. He's better working on his own than with a group. He likes to have his own territory and will chase off those who venture into it. He wants recognition for his work, but more practical rewards mean nothing to him.

Best Match with: Those who set clear boundaries, active women.
Bad Breed for: A boring partner.

TIBETAN TERRIER

If he doesn't walk like a Terrier and he doesn't talk like a Terrier, can he possibly be a Terrier? In this case, no. The Tibetan Terrier man is definitely a member of the Non-Sporting Dog Group. He has none of the Terrier's wild energy or work ethic. The Tibetan is capable of showing a wide range of behavior but, unlike the wildly unpredictable Doberman, he tends to live up to his partner's expectations of him. He'll be what you need him to be. (Perhaps its more correct to say that he'll be what you insist that he be.) If you let him dominate the relationship, he will. Better not. That's when his less-than-positive traits will emerge. At his best, he's charming and playful. At his worst, he's a ne'er-do-well.

Head: He's not intellectual, nor wildly talented, but what he lacks in talent, he makes up for with his willingness to please you. He'll learn what he needs to know in order to make you happy.

Heart: This man needs closeness. When you're out of town, he'll sleep with your old T-shirt next to his face at night. He just wants to smell you there. The Tibetan man is no extrovert and can be shy or aloof with strangers. He's a proud, sensitive soul, so don't put him down, especially in front of others.

Family: A better husband than father, he could do fine with an only child. Only children are usually well-behaved and tend to obey the household rules. This man will be miserable in a house full of noisy, messy, snot-nosed kids.

Work: He needs you to expect something of him, otherwise he could fritter his life away, or waste his energy in useless pursuits. He isn't driven to do any particular kind of work, but will apply himself to what he's given. Not inclined to put himself forward, he's better working for others than for himself. He'll need a regular schedule. The ideal job for a Tibetan man? Professional husband.

Best Match with: Lots of love… sometimes tough love.
Bad Breed for: Lots of kids, beraters and shamers

Porch Dogs and Mixed Breeds
All-American Mutts

THE PORCH DOG

The quintessential All-American Male, the Porch Dog is a one-man melting pot... a mixture of so many breeds that the traits of no single breed have dominance in his nature. He's the "dawg" of the Dog World... the big, sweet, lovable pooch on the porch. Everyone likes him, but no one knows exactly what he is.

While a PD's definitely loyal when he's with his partner, he will sniff a passing skirt or even stray from home if you're not vigilant. The good news? Porch Dogs always come home. He may not like the welcome he receives on his return, but he will come home.

Friendly, easygoing, likable, easy to please, the PD Man is happy at work, at play, or just relaxing. Though he may be smart as a whip, he's not always easy to train. Remember, he's got all those different breeds pulling him this way and that. He doesn't mean to be bad. Sometimes he just can't help himself. It's not the devil that makes him do it, it's that little bit of Basenji on his Mama's side. More even-keeled than a simple Mixed Breed, the Porch Dog's motto is: "Moderation in (almost) all things."

Who's my pick for the archetypal Porch Dog? The big dog himself... our forty-second president, Bill Clinton. Known for his moderate politics and his immoderate love life, he is widely acknowledged as our hardest-working president. That's the Working Dog in him. It's the lovable Sporting Dog that feels our pain, the Sight Hound that contributes its vision. Clinton's Herder helped him shine at those televised Town Meetings and his popularity ratings, even in the face of impeachment, attest to his ability to bring the rest of us along with him. It was the outgoing Hauling Dog that played saxophone on the Arsenio Show and that makes him so attractive to the opposite sex. And the Scent Hound? Well, we all know waaaaay too much about the Scent Hound. Luckily, he had enough Companion Dog to keep his family together and his Terrier traits compelled him to stick with the job, even in the face of horrifying adversity. Love him or hate him, he is the breed for all seasons.

MIXED BREEDS

Less moderate than the Porch Dog, the Mixed Breed is a blend of two different breeds. He's a Lab/Shepherd mix. He's a Beagle/Corgie mix. He's a, well… you get the point. The biggest problem you'll have with him is that you'll never know which breed you're going to get in a given situation. A Mixed Breed Man may be an interesting blend of mismatched qualities, or a real Jekyll and Hyde. Though Mixed Breeds can make wonderfully stimulating partners, some Breeds just don't mix well. While a Doberman might be great as the other half of a Poodle, he's no picnic mixed with a Giant Schnauzer or a Komondor. If you're a great match for a Pointer, but a bad match for an Irish Setter, your chance of finding happiness with a combination of the two are 50/50. Ask yourself, "Am I willing to be miserable half the time?" If the answer is no, don't pick that mix.

How do you know if your perfect match is a Mixed Breed? If you've taken the Women's Quiz and have come up with no good matches, your best match is most probably a Mixed Breed. If your man has taken the Men's Quiz and has come up with either wildly differing matches, or no match at all, he is very likely a Mixed Breed Man.

Section Two:
Choosing and Living with Your Match

Pick of the Litter:

How to Choose the Man, Once You've Chosen the Breed

Pick of the Litter

So... you've found your matching breed. Or maybe you're a good match with several different breeds. The next step is choosing the individual man. Of course, you'll want the pick of the litter.

Where to find him...

If I were talking about real dogs, I'd tell you to find a responsible breeder. Finding your Dog-Man will, of course, be a little more complicated. Where you'll find him will depend completely on the breed you're looking for and the Dog Group that breed belongs to.

Terriers are workaholics. You'll find yours at the office or somewhere on the job. Look for a guy in a suit and running shoes, sprinting down the street with a cell phone in one hand and a briefcase in the other, his power tie flying behind him. You may have to trip him to get his attention. You might also take a business course at night. The Terrier will be that intense guy in class, with the brilliant plan to market fat suits to anorexics. He'll make you believe he can actually pull it off. Before the last class, he'll have hundreds of orders. The worst way to meet a Terrier? Pull into his parking spot, just as he's preparing to make his turn.

Herding Dog Men are every bit as intense as Terriers, but are less likely to be found working alone. Wherever you see a Herder, he'll be leading others. This guy lives for those weekend office retreats where he and his co-workers play cooperative games, learn about win-win negotiating, and engage in trust exercises. You can find your Herder coaching a ball team, organizing a community project, or (as CEO of a large corporation) in a fancy corner office. He may be an officer in one of the armed services. Unfortunately, he may also be an Amway Salesman, or the Jehovah's Witness that knocks on your door every weekend. He won't let up until you're selling soap or Heaven or both! Since both Herders and Terriers have obsessive, often addictive personalities, you may run into either at a Twelve-Step meeting.

You're more likely to find a Sight Hound in an art class or a jazz club. He may even be an artist or a musician. If you want to meet him, try frequenting museums and galleries. Lurk around your local coffee shop and look for an interesting man with a sketchbook. Buy tickets to the opera. This man is a visionary, so you may also meet him on a meditation retreat, or at a lecture on Spirituality and Quantum Physics, or heading an effort to introduce predators back into the wild. Whatever he's interested in, make sure it's something that interests you. Don't pretend to be more spiritual or artistic than you really are. Sight Hounds can spot a phony several miles away.

Look for Scent Hounds any place that groups of men congregate... ball stadiums, sports bars, tractor pulls, Sturgis. Or arrange to witness a robbery. As many Hounds are attracted to police work, you're almost certain to meet one while paging through mug shots at the precinct house. Thinking about changing your job? Your hound may be a corporate headhunter or work for an employment agency. And this is a man who will actually marry a girl he meets in a bar.

Working Dogs are family men, upstanding members of the community who define themselves by their ability to make a living. You may meet your Worker match at your church or synagogue. You might also try the local Chamber of Commerce breakfast, or the groundbreaking ceremony for the new community center. He's the big, smiling guy selling lottery tickets for the Lions Club. Get a friend or family member to set you up on a date.

While Working Dog Men tend to be a conservative lot, a subset of the group can be found further out on the social limb. We're talking about the Hauling Dogs. A Hauler loves a party and is the first to arrive and last to leave. He'll be the only man singing at the karioke bar who's actually entertaining. Got a vacation coming up? Try an "extreme" experience… cliff climbing, skydiving, or snowboarding down a glacier. There's bound to be a Hauler in your group.

You'll have to work a little harder to find your Companion Dog Man. Men of this group tend to stay close to home. Try attending that series of readings, sponsored by your local bookstore. Or take up jogging through nearby neighborhoods and look for the man who's mulching his well-cared-for azalea bushes. You may want to take out a personals ad. He'll be the one who really does enjoy walks on the beach and long nights chatting by the fire. Though he won't be attracted to national politics, you can often find your Companion Man down at the town board meeting, arguing with neighbors about variances and local zoning laws.

In contrast to the Companion, the Sporting Dog Man is out and about. In the summer he's running in the park, swimming at the lake, or out chasing a ball almost anywhere. In the winter he's cross-country skiing or on the track at the YMCA. If you're invited to a friend's backyard barbecue, you should certainly go. You're sure to find a Sporting Man there, especially if your friend has a trampoline or a swimming pool. And go to every wedding you're invited to. An unusual number of handsome groomsmen are Sporting Dog Men.

Non-Sporting Dog Men are hard to pin down. Because the breeds in this group are so different from one another, it's impossible to generalize about where you might find them. You'll need to carefully look at the description of your matching breed and figure out for yourself where you might go to meet him.

Unless he's truly awful, give him a second date.

Okay. You met him, you went out, and it was less than a perfect evening. First of all, we're trying to break our old dating patterns. Many women are wildly attracted to men who are wrong for them and feel ho-hum about Mr. Right. If you think this may be true of you, try not to judge any man by your first impression. Lots of men are nervous on a first date.

Take the case of Alan, a prime example of a first date disaster. Alan is a really nice Terrier Man. He's quite attractive and very intelligent, but his love life is a mess. All of Alan's friends are constantly trying to help him by setting him up on blind dates. Several of these I witnessed, first-hand, and so became familiar with his self-sabotaging behavior. Here's the basic scenario: As soon as Alan is introduced to an attractive woman, he goes into a manic Terrier spin. He can't calm down long enough to even ask the woman what she does for a living. He just launches into a date-long, high-speed monologue, usually involving major league baseball and the Beatles. In true Terrier form, he digs himself into a hole, buries himself, and never gets a second date. This is sad because, given a second chance, he would eventually calm down and turn into the reasonable human being I know him to be. Alan is a real catch, disguised as a reject.

Breed Rescue

Speaking of rejects: Some of the very best dogs can be gotten from Breed Rescue groups. These dogs tend to be older, already trained, and very grateful that you've stepped in to save them from a life of loneliness. The human equivalent of the Breed Rescue Dog is the previously married man. Just because a man has been divorced, it doesn't mean he's a bad man. He may only have been a bad match for the woman he chose to marry. Statistics tell us that men who have been married once are more likely to want to marry again. And studies have shown that second and third marriages are usually better marriages, as both parties go into them with more reasonable expectations. If you have children from a previous marriage, you should understand that men with their own children will probably be more accepting of yours. If you have kids, try joining a group for single parents. There are always lots of single dads at school picnics and soccer matches. I even know one single dad who met his soon-to-be-second wife at the Laundromat!

Before you say, "I do," meet his family.

We all show only our best side to a new love interest. Want to know what lies beneath a man's best side? Then arrange to meet his family. With certain breeds it is imperative that you do this, while other breeds are a safe bet no matter what kind of craziness they grew up with. You can take a chance with the Spaniel, but it's better to know ahead of time that your Doberman has two brothers in prison and a mother on America's Most Wanted. Pay attention to those red flags when they jump out at you.

Is he housebroken?

If you're the kind of woman who likes her house just so, there are some breeds you should steer clear of no matter how compatible you are with him in other areas. If you're looking for long-term love, you'll have to be able to live with him. Visit his home. Drop in unannounced. Talk to his mother. Go away for the weekend with him. Check out his suitcase. Is it full of balled-up, wrinkled shirts and dirty underwear, or are his clothes neatly folded? Does he drop his towels on the bathroom floor or does he hang them up? Does he leave the top off the toothpaste and hair in the sink? If you're thinking his little tidiness problem will fix itself once you have the rock on your finger, you'll need another think. Within days of the wedding vows, you will mutate into his mother and he will be fantasizing about running away from home. Some people just do not care that the house is messy. If you do care, find someone who feels the same way. It is also good to remember that, with dogs, some seem to be wantonly destructive, while others merely shed. There is a big difference between a man who leaves his socks on the coffee table and one who'll break your Haviland china, one precious piece at a time.

Submissiveness Test:

When picking a puppy, a prospective buyer should hold him on his back to see how long he will remain calm. This is a way to test for submissiveness. A puppy that struggles to free himself immediately will constantly be struggling for control and will, therefore, be harder to train. While we cannot, for obvious reasons, do this test with men, there are ways to test for the human equivalent. Start slowly, giving him things to react to. Wear a color he doesn't like. Ask if you can drive his car. Borrow one of his CD's without asking. Be the aggressor in bed. Call him for a date. Get the point? If you need a man who can go with the flow, test him before you commit. If he freaks when he sees you wearing his T-shirt, just imagine sharing a life with him!

Remember...

What you can tolerate while dating may become intolerable once you're forced to wake up with it every single morning. No matter who you are, or how great your powers of persuasion, you won't be able to change his basic nature. Though you can, on occasion, teach an old dog a new trick, you can't turn a Pointer into a Pug.

BAD DOG!

BAD DOG!

There is an old saying that goes… "There are no bad dogs, just bad dog owners." And there's more than a little truth in this saying. A dog of any breed can be a good dog, if he's handled correctly, and even the mildest breed may turn on you if he's been raised wrong or treated badly. The same can be said of men. Though there are some cases in which a man seems to have been "born bad," and has remained that way throughout his life, there are many more in which nurture has triumphed over nature. Similarly, there are those very sad cases in which a loving, cheerful child has been altered by the events of his life, becoming a bitter, cynical, or violent man.

We do have a measure of control, however. Though you can't change a man's basic nature, you can influence his behavior, for better or for worse. There are some basic rules to follow if you're looking for that positive outcome.

Pit Bulls were bred to be fighting dogs. They have extremely strong jaws and an instinct to dominate. Since Pit Bull men have this same aggressive nature and dominant personality, giving them free run and no limits is a very bad idea. This goes for Pit Bull kids as well as husbands. If you have a testosterone-filled fourteen-year-old with poor impulse control, a propensity for aggressive behavior, no supervision, and access to an unlocked gun rack, you don't need Miss Cleo to tell you that something bad is going to happen. And when the inevitable does happen, is it the Pit Bull's fault? It's not quite that simple. New laws are holding parents responsible for the actions of violent kids, and rightfully so.

There are good reasons you should meet the family of the Rottweiler you're dating. Some personality types are just plain prone to problems when they're not raised properly. In the same vein, even the well-bred man will have very particular needs, each according to his type. If you don't have lots of time and a bottomless well of energy, don't take on an extremely high-maintenance breed. Let's face it, a Border Collie man with nothing to do all day is going to rip the carpet out of your house. He can't help himself. It's written in his genes. If you've absolutely got to have him, you'll need to give him lots of attention. Otherwise, he'll find ways to entertain himself and you may not appreciate his choice of entertainment.

And it's not just the Border Collie. Any Herding Dog Man is going to be trouble when it comes time to retire from his job. It's bad enough when he has made his own decision to retire. If he is forced to retire, he will drive you absolutely mad. Let's say your Australian Shepherd husband takes an early retirement from the Marine Corps. If you haven't prepared for this ahead of time, by finding him something meaningful to do, get used to having a male shadow and hearing a daily chorus of "What'r ya doin'? Where ya goin'? Who'r ya talkin' to?" Your golden years are suddenly looking more like tarnished brass.

Men in the Working Dog Group can be just as much trouble as the Herders, but for completely different reasons. While less "workaholic" than their Herding Dog cousins, Working Dogs judge themselves by their ability to protect and support their families. A Working Dog who's been laid off, or fired from his job, is a miserable human being. He can quickly lose his confidence and sense of self. Rather than nipping at your heels and working your nerves, he may retreat into himself and sink into a deep depression. You'll come home at the end of your hard day to find him slumped in front of the tube, wearing a dirty flannel shirt and three-day growth of beard, and watching old Baretta reruns. If you don't find him something useful to do (and fast!) he could quietly drift away.

The rules for keeping a man happy (and in line) vary from group to group and breed to breed. Use your common sense. Has your Scent Hound husband started running with a pack of recently divorced womanizers he's met at the local Hooters? Don't demand that he stay in every night (a Scent Hound needs his pack), but you can quickly steer him to poker night with a group of happily married husbands. There are, of course, other options. You can move to another town, pay his new pals to dump him, or start looking for a good divorce lawyer.

If you're raising a brilliantly creative Sight Hound kid, don't offer him pot when he's twelve and think he's going to learn control down the road. A Sight Hound is already lost in his own head most of the time. You throw drugs into the mix and your budding creative genius may never be able to find his way out. We've all seen those headlines in the tabloids. And we've heard the Sight Hound's fans lament, "He was such a great actor, when he wasn't in jail."

Here's another recipe for growing a bad dog from a promising pup. Take a scrappy Bull Terrier kid from the streets, a kid with no real family support. Pump him up on steroids, throw him into a boxing ring and praise him for pummeling other guys in the head. Then reward his violent behavior with barrels of cash, while making sure he receives no real education. Remind you of anyone?

Let's be fair. There are as many "bad dogs" among sensitive artists as there are among strong-willed jocks. Of course, there is a big difference between catching your puppy as he pees on the carpet and watching helplessly as your attack dog eats off the neighbor's face. Some breeds of men are going to be, by their very nature, more dangerous than other breeds. While an intelligent, neurotic man may take a toll on your self-esteem, a big violent hunk could send you on a permanent vacation to the afterlife.

"But that won't happen to me!" some of you are saying right now, "I picked a sweet-natured, fun-loving Sporting Dog Man. He loves to do for me, and I never boss him." Yes, Retrievers love to fetch, but if his life becomes an endless series of trips to the market, the dry cleaners, the post office, and the drug store, you will wake up one day to find he has fallen for his oh-so-attentive little secretary. A Sporting Dog Man needs to have fun and, more importantly, he needs to be appreciated for all that errand running. He may never exhibit the "bad dog" traits that can (and should) frighten you in the more dominant groups, but he'll be a miserable mutt to live with, if you let his life become drudgery.

Just because they're easy to catch, doesn't mean they're easy to keep! The greatest sex in the world won't keep a Hauling Dog at home all the time. As soon as you put up the picket fence and give him a curfew, it won't matter if you look like Hallie Berry; your Husky will have hit the road with a truck stop waitress named Yvonne.

Why are we all shocked and amazed when we hear that our favorite sportscaster is a sex-obsessed control freak with a cross-dressing fetish? Gee, how could that have happened?

Easy. You only need one little, high-strung Terrier who likes to run with the Sporting Dogs. Put that little Terrier on national television every night, so that he becomes a celebrity (and all the girls who wouldn't date him in high school are suddenly interested), then surround him with macho athletes in a sexually charged atmosphere. What have you got? You've still got yourself a great sportscaster... when he's not too busy defending himself in court.

Just in case you're thinking none of this applies to you because you're always attracted to mild-mannered Companion Dog types... listen up. There's a little thing called shy-sharp syndrome. It can be triggered wherever there's a conflict between a timid dog and a dominant owner... or, for our purposes, between a domineering woman and her very gentle man. Bullying a submissive dog may cause him to turn and snap at you. Bullying a submissive man can have consequences you aren't prepared for. Yes, your husband may be a cuddly lap dog, but don't mistake passive for pushover. Sure, you can berate or nag at him constantly and he probably won't beat you. In the best case scenario, he'll find nasty little passive-aggressive ways to undermine you. In the worst case, he'll wait until you're asleep and spike your Tylenol with arsenic. If you love your lap dog, lighten up. As a rule, those timid types don't fair too well in prison.

So what does all this mean? No one's telling you not to marry that adorable Basenji, or that you should dump your sexy Weimaraner. You just need to know the nature of your beast. Divorce courts, like animal shelters, are the final destination for women who thought they could change the nature of their companions. But hey, don't take my advice. Go ahead and marry that Dober-Man, even though you divorced three of his breed before you met him. You can change this one with the transforming power of love, right?

Get a grip, girlfriend! As Dr Phil might say ... "How's that working for you?"

Avoiding Mr. Wrong

Avoiding Mr. Wrong

The best man can have his worst brought out by the wrong mate. Yet some women seem compelled to seek out relationships with Mr. Wrong. If you're one of these women, you simply cannot go on gut instinct when it comes to hooking up with a man. It's actually a pretty simple rule. Just figure out which breeds you cannot live with and avoid them like the plague. If you insist on choosing the wrong breed, it's certain you'll end up torturing some perfectly nice guy who is only trying to be himself.

The truth is that women often want their men to change and men never want their women to change. Think about it. How often have you heard some poor perplexed man say, "I don't know what happened! She was happy being a housewife, then all of a sudden she felt unfulfilled and got a job!" A man is almost certain to use the words "all of a sudden" when describing a change in a girlfriend or wife. It's as though he has had no warning at all. All the complaining, the tears, the dreaded late night talks mean nothing. She's just in a mood. She'll get over it. And if, instead, she does something drastic, it's always an unpleasant surprise. If the average man marries a pretty blonde cheerleader, he'll be just thrilled if she very gradually becomes a pretty old cheerleader. Of course, women know that there is no such thing as a pretty old cheerleader. Men don't.

Harder than getting a man to accept change in you, is getting him to change his own behavior. The very act of trying to change him may start a pattern that will transform your relationship into a nightmare. But don't despair. You can make life easier just by avoiding a disastrous match.

241

As a rule, Workers, Herders and Terrier Men need a woman who can stand up for herself and stand up to them. This does not mean browbeating or dominating. The worst matches for most breeds in these three groups include both doormats and ball-busters. In order to share your life with a dominant man, you'll need high self-esteem and confidence, tempered with a good nature and patience. If you know when to stand your ground and when to back down, one of these men might just be perfect for you. But if you don't pick your battles wisely, your life will resemble a grudge match on the World Wrestling Championships. One of you will be carried out of the ring. And if you never stand up to your dominant breed at all? Get used to wiping the bootprints off your back. It takes an Alpha woman to deal with an Alpha man.

Of course, a man doesn't have to be a high testosterone type to be a bad match for you. We've heard so many women express the following: " I want a sensitive, highly intelligent, and artistic man, who also makes an incredible amount of money." Don't delude yourself. There are only a handful of these men in the world. Most of them are already dating supermodels and the rest are dating other men. So, if money and stability mean everything to you, do not pair up with a Sight Hound. The Sight Hound is a man who is dedicated to his vision, whether or not that vision ever makes him any bucks. He needs a woman who will support him in this and take him "for richer, for poorer." If you expect the artist with the faraway eyes to suddenly don a three-piece suit and go to work for Morgan Stanley, you're living in la-la land. He'll pack up and move to Woodstock, and you'll be sitting in your Manhattan apartment staring at an empty easel.

If rowdy, boisterous, rough-and-tumble boys attract you, you probably date a lot of Scent Hound Men. Think you want to marry one? Are you prepared to weed out his trouble-making buddies? Do you have the confidence to deal with his roving eye? While frat parties can be fun while you're in college, will you be able to handle them well into your sixties? The nature of the Scent Hound Man is particularly strong and you will never be able to change it. Argue and he'll dig in. Complain and he'll turn a deaf ear. Berate him and he'll simply run down to his local watering hole to hang out with his pals. Fence him in and you'll be filling out a missing persons report, while he's hit the road with a Grrl Band drummer named Princess Die. A needy, clinging, suspicious mate is a Scent Hound's idea of hell. And unlike some of the other groups, Scent Hound Men do not stick around when they're unhappy. Still, the worst match of all for a Scent Hound is an elitist or snob. If you turn up your nose at an evening of bowling, he could retaliate by inviting Princess Die to your perfect little dinner party.

If you're a world traveler, a workaholic, or a woman who needs a lot of time alone, please stay away from breeds in the Companion Group. As a rule, Companion Men are for women who dream of a quiet life of togetherness, with a dependable partner. He gardens with you, cuddles with you, and his pending retirement won't weigh on you like a backpack full of bricks. He's always liked to hang around home so there won't be any dramatic change when he hits age sixty-five. Speaking of dramatic changes, your Companion Man avoids them like the plague. He doesn't like change. If you're a woman who feels the need to constantly change your hair, your job, and your living room furniture, you need to know that this will upset him. Finally, if you're a screamer, or an unusually forceful or critical woman, you could make your mellow Companion mate turn mean. Remember? It's called Shy-Sharp Syndrome. When your normally sweet-natured Companion has had all the nagging he can take, he may turn and snap at you.

"Aren't there some men who are a good match with almost anyone?" you may well ask. "What about the Sporting Dogs?"

Yes, Sporting Dog Men are extremely good-natured and loving, but don't go near the Sporting Breeds unless you really enjoy outdoor activity, weekend getaways and lots of company. These men thrive on fun and adventure, family and friends. If you're a sad sack, a cynic, or a loner, you can see a therapist, but please don't see a Sporting Dog Man. And if you have a tendency toward bossiness, don't ever marry one. You'll get bossier as time progresses, while he deflates like an old balloon. So don't even start with him. The world has enough formerly fun-loving Sporting Men who have had all the joy sucked out of them by depressives and women with control issues. Easygoing, in-the-moment, go-with-the-flow gals are the best partners for these great guys.

I can't repeat this often enough: There are no bad dogs. But if you choose badly and try, after the fact, to change your man, you may end up with something that feels very bad indeed. In the world of dogs, if you treat a Silky like a Doberman, you'll end up with a mean-spirited, snappy, passive-aggressive lap dog that bites your ankles and pees on your Pradas. The same holds true for men. Deal appropriately with the nature of your Beast and you will come out looking like Beauty.

Dogs in the Office

Dogs in the Office

Congratulations! You've met and married the dog of your dreams and everything is peachy at home. Your Harrier is happy. Your Cairn is calm. Your Dalmatian is doting and docile and all is right with the world. Until, Monday morning rolls around and you have to schlep off to work and deal with that sadistic Giant Schnauzer in the big corner office. Or maybe, your problem is the tyrannical Terrier in the cubicle next to yours. Perhaps you've worked your way all the way up the corporate ladder, but are concerned about that bullheaded Border Collie your company just hired. Just when you figured out one breed, you're faced with dozens more. They're everywhere and nothing has prepared you for this.

Calm down, darling. You're about to get a crash course on dogs in the office. As I've explained, you won't be able to change any of them. But you can learn to understand them better, so that you can deal with them more effectively. Though it may be impossible to get your male co-workers to actually take the Porch Dogs Quiz, some breeds are so recognizable that you won't need the test to tell you who they are.

A Herding Dog Man will constantly call meetings. He'll call a meeting for 7:00 am, or during your lunch break, or even several hours after work's supposed to end for the day. And he'll make you feel that you absolutely have to be at the meeting. He won't understand that little Justin is graduating from kindergarten this afternoon and you have to be there, recording it for posterity. A Herder doesn't own a video camera, unless he uses it for work, in which case it will be glued to him and only shut off when he has to change the battery. When he's not scheduling meetings, a Herder's out organizing the company softball team, or planning the company picnic. This man's co-workers are his friends. He won't understand if you don't feel the same way.

Terriers are not subtle. Neither are they tactful. You do not want a Terrier Man in any job that requires that he consider the feelings of others. An editor friend found out the hard way when she hired a terrier as her assistant. Her reasoning? He was smart, insightful, and he loved to work. He worked long hours, and never thought to ask for overtime pay. There was just one tiny problem. Shortly after the Terrier was hired, several of her best freelance writers disappeared. When she called them, they were never available. And they never called her. After making inquiries, she was informed that writers don't respond well to being told that their work "reeks." The resourceful editor managed to wrangle a horizontal promotion for her assistant, moving him out of the Creative department and into Production, where his Terrier qualities were appreciated.

A Sight Hound Man will be terrific in the Creative department, but will most likely be a washout in Production or Sales. Most Sight Hounds have the look of someone who was dropped on the planet by benign aliens and frequently contacts the Mother Ship. If communiqués from the Mother Ship begin to take precedence over memos from your desk, you may have a problem on your hands. If you push him too hard, he will slam out the door, screaming something about irreconcilable creative differences. If you don't push at all, he'll be off and running down a path you may not like. This is definitely a man who marches to the beat of his own drum. That beat may be a polka or it may be a mambo. Figure out which before you hire him.

Scent Hounds can mean trouble for the women who share their workplace. A Scent Hound almost always goes out with the guys after work. He's the man who'll steal your client by switching the meeting to a strip club without informing you. You'll be sitting alone at an empty conference table. They'll be watching a naked woman gyrate on a cocktail table. The Scent Hound may well sign your client and the boss will never remember that you're the one who found him in the first place. The client, who read the small print through a haze of alcohol and the pink glow of sex, may live to regret the deal. Unlike your superiors, he will remember you.

Both charming and good at what they do, Sporting Dog Men are people persons. Hire them for any job that requires well-developed social skills and the ability to hunt things down, or flush them out of hiding. Remember that while these men are good workers, work is not their first priority. A job is what this man does in order to finance his real life… the time he spends with his hobbies, favorite sports, family, and friends. If you load him down with overtime or force him to take work home from the office, you may lose a valuable employee. This is the guy that flex time was invented for.

Companion Dog Men fall into two categories, good-natured and rather shy fellows, or aggressive little ankle-biters. If you have both in your accounting office, send the former to placate the IRS, and assign the latter to collect delinquent payments. Under no circumstances should you reverse their job assignments. Neither of these two types is your deal closer. The one is too reserved and the other too irritating. You'll end up with a deal you don't want, or no deal at all. Above all, don't sell your Companion Man short. He's very good at what he does. He just isn't your front man.

The Working Dogs are a mixed bag. Though all of them define themselves by their work, some are less predictable than others. In almost any job, a Newfie or Saint Bernard Man is worth his considerable weight in gold. But if you work for the police department investigative unit, you may have to assign a German Shepherd to keep an eye on some of your Rottweilers. And what about that guy in the next cubicle who's constantly flirting with you? If he's flirting with other women in the office he's probably just a Hauling Dog and completely harmless. If he's bee-lined in on you, and you're getting a creepy feeling, you may be dealing with a Komondor. In that case, may we suggest you report him to the nearest German Shepherd?

Non-Sporting Dog Men also vary widely in type. Some, given explicit instructions and a firm schedule, make excellent employees. With a few exceptions, these are not men you put in charge of a large project, or choose to head up the new department. They don't define themselves by work, like the Working Dogs, or feel the need to lead others, like the Herders. Neither do they have the vision of the Sight Hounds, or the drive of the Terriers. And while Sporting Dog Men tend to be very good at the one thing they do, Non-Sporting Men tend to be dabblers. He'll drift into a job, learning exactly as much as he needs in order to get that job done.

Know Your Dog:
Advice for the Married Woman

Know Your Dog:
Advice for the Married Woman

So... you've found your matching dog and it's not your husband's breed. It may even be that your husband's breed is the very worst breed you could've hooked up with. I'm not going to tell you to get a restraining order or to pack his things and leave them out on the curb. In fact, this chapter is for women who don't want a new relationship but simply desire a greater understanding of their husbands.

The very worst mistake a woman can make is to try and force her man to behave like a member of another breed or dog group. We're initially attracted to our Sight Hound's vision. Then, after a few months of togetherness, we begin to feel cheated because he isn't as fun loving as a Sporting Dog Man. We're happy about the fact that our Herder makes a good living, but the very qualities that make this possible drive us crazy when we're trying to relax with him. When we try to force the Sight Hound to lighten up, or the Herder to relax, we are struggling against reality. A large part of the misery in any relationship springs from this struggle, not from the original complaint.

So stop struggling, take a deep breath, and look honestly at your partner. Decide which behaviors are innate in the breed and which are merely bad habits that can be modified by training. Learn to pick your battles, confining them to areas where some change may actually be possible.

Most Terriers, many Herders, and even some Working Dog Men, like the Rottweiler or the Giant Schnauzer, are just not cuddlers. They have a hard time relaxing and are happiest when involved in some sort of work or hobby. These men can also lack tact. If you ask a Terrier whether or not you look fat in your expensive new dress, he may just say, "Yes." On the positive side, he isn't likely to lie to you. And most Herders and Terriers keep themselves too busy to have time for an affair. Here's a suggestion: If you're married to one of these guys and you need more affection, find a good masseuse, call a nurturing friend, visit your Grandmother, get a puppy, or all of the above. Let this guy off the hug hook.

Perhaps you've married a loving Spaniel or a loyal Worker, like the Newfie or the Bernese Mountain Dog. He gives you all the hugs and cuddles a woman could ever want, but ask for a little space and you'll have a desperate man on your hands. It just isn't in him to back away. Instead of asking him to stop doing something (i.e. hanging around you), give him something positive to do. Send your Retriever off to the grocery with a long list. Put your Worker to work building that dream house in the country. Send the Spaniel off to the park with the kids. Screaming, "If you don't get away from me I'm going to lose my mind" will only hurt his feelings and will never get the results you want. He'll be afraid he's losing you, which will make him more likely to stick to you like flypaper.

Falling in love with a Companion or a laid-back Non-Sporting breed may have seemed like a good idea when you were young and so very sure that money could never buy happiness. Then, of course, you woke up. You found you were living in the real world. All of a sudden your needs have changed and he hasn't. If you want to keep your husband and buy that new BMW, you're going to have to go out and earn the money yourself. That's your only option. Don't beat this man up because you've suddenly decided you're the material girl.

Small problems in a marriage often become large problems when a man reaches retirement age. If your hubby's a Herder, a Worker, or a Terrier, you have absolutely got to plan ahead. Sign your Herder up to coach Little League. Draw up those plans for your dream house and give them to your Worker. Nominate your Terrier to the board of your condo association. You won't have many friends in the building, but the elevators will be running and the chlorine levels in the pool will be checked frequently.

Most Twelve-Step groups emphasize the fact that we can't change the behavior of another person, we can only change our own behavior. If you're a timid woman married to a dominant breed, you'll have to learn to stand up to him, or get used to being his permanent doormat. Unless you change your ways, he'll have no reason to change his. These same self-help groups begin their meetings with the Serenity Prayer: "God, grant me the courage to change the things that I can change, the serenity to accept the things I can't change, and the wisdom to know the difference." When dealing with a difficult breed, this is the only position to take.

Section III:
QUIZZES AND SCORING

Taking the Porch Dogs Quiz

The Porch Dogs Quiz has two parts. The first part contains questions for the woman to answer. The second is for her male partner, assuming there is one. They are:

Women's Quiz: Dog of My Dreams
(or... What kind of man is right for me?)

Men's Quiz: A Matter of Breeding
(or... What sort of dog am I?)

Before you read another word, you should stop and complete your section of the Porch Dogs Quiz. (Or take the computerized Quiz at our web site: **www.porchdogs.com**)

DON'T CHEAT!

If you know why you're being asked a certain question, it may affect your answer and, therefore, your results.

Okay. Now that you've taken the Quiz, we'll explain to you how this works. I've given each breed of dog a rating of 1-5 in each of 16 categories. These categories include traits like dominance, learning rate, emotional stability, territoriality, and activity level (both indoor and outdoor activity). We have related each of these canine traits to a quality found in the human male. For example, problem-solving ability in the dog breed relates to IQ in the man, canine guarding behavior corresponds to the human male's level of possessiveness. High dominance with other dogs (other men, for our purposes) roughly translates as competitiveness and a tendency to jealousy, while high dominance within the family can be read as bossiness. It isn't always clear-cut. A high score in outdoor activity may mean your guy is a marathon runner, or it may mean he's always at the office, depending on how he scores in other areas.

I have divided the sixteen traits into four indexes. The Emotional Index includes Emotional Openness, Emotional Stability, Extroversion, and a trait I call "Good with Kids." Intellect, Cooperation, Predictability, and Learning Rate are traits in the Intelligence Index. In the Energy Index, we find Indoor Activity, Outdoor Activity, Vitality (as opposed to Gentleness), and level of Alertness, which is a measure of mental energy. The traits in the Dominance Index are Dominance (with other men), Bossiness (within the family), Territoriality and Guarding Behavior.

The questions in the women's quiz will establish the levels of each trait a woman needs, or can tolerate, in a partner. The men's quiz questions should tell us the levels of these traits exhibited by the man taking the quiz. A man can locate his breed and a woman can find her best matching breed by using the Trait Charts in the back of the book. Comparing the outcome of the two quizzes will tell you if a woman and her man are a good match.

About the Women's Quiz

The Women's Quiz is a personality test and your answers to the questions will determine which breed of man is actually right for you. Very often, the men who are right for us are not the men we are drawn to. Using the information gathered in this part of the quiz, you can help yourself to recognize Mr. Right when you meet him.

After taking the quiz and scoring your answers, turn to the Trait Charts in the back of the book to find your best match. If you are married, or involved in a relationship, have your man take the Men's Quiz and compare your results with his.

Women's Quiz: Dog of My Dreams

The easiest and most accurate way to take the quiz is to do the online version at **www.porchdogs.com.** To take the printed version, simply jot down the letter that appears beside the most appropriate answer for each question.

It is important to answer the questions honestly. Go with your first instinct, or think of how you have tended to behave in previous relationships. Do not answer according to how you would "like" to behave or you will end up with a false match. If the question asks about your "husband" and you are unmarried, simply substitute the word "boyfriend" or "date" in your mind.

1)   **Which of these song lyrics best describes your love-making style?**

    a)   "C'mon, Baby, twist and shout!"
    b)   "Rock me, Baby, rock me all night long."
    c)   "Love me tender, love me true."

2)   **Finish the following statement. My favorite thing to do on a rainy Sunday afternoon is …**

    a)   Find the nearest mall or gym! I can't just sit inside all day.
    b)   Use the time inside to organize and get the house in shape.
    c)   Pajamas, a good book and a cup of tea.

3)   **Your friends have just invited you and your guy for a weekend camping trip. You're thrilled when your guy responds with the following:**

    a)   "Tents? Who needs tents? After the 10 mile hike, I'll build us a shelter out of tree bark, then catch a fish with my bare hands."
    b)   "Sound like fun. I'll bring my dome tent, hibachi, air mattress and the portable TV."
    c)   "Camping? Remind me again why these people are our friends?

4) You and your man are supposed to be leaving for a long weekend at the beach, but he shows up Friday PM with a load of work from the office... again! What's your response?

a) I suggest that he go with me, but take his laptop and cell phone along.

b) I tell him that a break will improve his efficiency. We'll go for two days and he can work on the third.

c) I express concern for his health and plead with him to go without the work.

5) Some old friends of yours come to town and invite you and your partner out to dinner. The friends are very witty and your guy has trouble keeping up with the conversation. What do you do?

a) Try to help him negotiate the rough waters. My friends could make anyone feel like a dolt.

b) Let him deal with it. If I'm enjoying my friends, I haven't even noticed him struggling.

c) I feel very embarrassed and, when he leaves the table, I quickly blurt out his other good qualities to my friends.

6) You are allergic to perfume, but every year at Christmas, for three years in a row, your man has given you bath products that are loaded with perfume. You feel..?

  a) Thankful to have such a sweet man, even though he has a memory like a sieve.

  b) Baffled. How could he keep forgetting? Is he repressing negative feelings toward me?

  c) Irritated. How many times do I have to remind him? If he cared about me, he'd remember something this important.

7) Your neat-freak parents just called to say they're popping in for a surprise visit. The house is a mess and your live-in guy tells you he's supposed to meet his friends at the gym for a workout session. What do you expect him to do?

  a) Ditch the guys, wash those dishes and stay to greet the folks.

  b) Help out a bit before he leaves for his workout at the appointed time.

  c) Go to his workout. They're not his parents and I really do this better without him hanging around and getting in the way.

8) **If my husband came home and, out of the blue, announced that he had quit his job, I would feel...**

    a) A little nervous, but excited. This could be the start of a whole new life.

    b) Worried, but, hey! It's his life and I don't want a miserable husband. We'll get by... I hope.

    c) Fearful. I thought I knew my husband and could count on him not to do anything crazy.

9) **Your man has been moody and uncommunicative. When you ask him what's wrong, he says he doesn't want to talk about it. What's your reaction?**

    a) Fine with me. The last thing I want is some "Woody Allen" type who whines about his problems all the time.

    b) I'd become a cheerleader, trying to "jolly" him out of his bad mood.

    c) I'd imagine worst case scenarios, then wheedle, cajole, and threaten, trying every tactic until I got the truth out of him.

10) When it comes to having children, which of the following TV shows best fits your ideal of family?

    a) Malcolm in the Middle – a bunch of kids, a little chaos, and a lot of fun.

    b) Leave it to Beaver – two kids and a spouse with a good job.

    c) Dharma and Greg – a really cute guy and no kids… at least not for now.

11) You've received an invitation to your high school reunion. Since you don't have a husband or a date, you decide to hire an escort for the evening. Which of the following do you choose?

    a) Someone who'll stick by me and who won't embarrass me, or draw too much attention to himself.

    b) Someone who is socially at ease enough to dance with me, converse with strangers and help me get through the evening.

    c) A guy that everyone will notice, with enough of the actor in him to play a successful husband or doting fiancé.

12) **You're having what you think is a friendly disagreement with your guy when, all of a sudden, he blows up and insults you personally. Which is closest to your reaction?**

    a)   I'm so shocked and hurt, that I run to the car and drive away in tears.

    b)   I'm shocked. I did nothing to deserve that. If he thinks he's getting any sex for the next month, he can think again!

    c)   I give him an earful, then let it roll off my back. Everybody has the right to a bad day and a moment of poor judgement.

13) **Finish the following statement: If I never find a life partner…**

    a)   I may be lonely, but I'll still make enough money to do fine on my own.

    b)   I'll get by, but may have to scrimp and will certainly have to do without some luxuries.

    c)   Is there a market for elderly prostitutes?

14) **Finish the following statement: When my man orders me around...**

  a) It'll be a cold day in hell!

  b) I sit him down and explain why his behavior is unacceptable.

  c) I laugh and continue doing what I was doing, the way I was doing it.

15) **Your new boyfriend is moving in and insists on bringing all his old furniture with him. He's completely attached to it, but it's sooooo not you. How do you handle it?**

  a) Let him bring it, but gradually wheedle it away from him, one ugly piece at a time.

  b) Sweetly suggest the two of us go shopping for some new furniture together.

  c) Make the best of it. Sometimes old and ugly can be looked on as eclectic.

16) **If my boyfriend or spouse became horribly jealous of my close male friends, I would...**

  a) Simply not tell him when I planned to see one of my friends.

  b) Be slightly flattered, but insist that my friends remain my friends.

  c) Probably see my friends less often and only when he was with me. They are less important than he is.

17) **When it comes to a cheating spouse, which animal's behavior best describes your attitude?**

    a)   A wounded bird, crushed and broken.
    b)   A black widow… literally.
    c)   A female wolf. I mate for life, but can make his life very unpleasant.
    d)   A hyena. I'm dominant enough to run the other females off.
    e)   A bat, blissfully blind to whatever may be going on.
    f)   A goose. What's good for the gander is good for me!

18) **Rate the following in numerical order, from most true (5) to least true (1): "When I think about aging, it frightens me to think that I might…**

    a)   End up old, broke, and unable to support myself."
    b)   Lose my ability to think clearly."
    c)   End up spending my final years alone and lonely, with no one to love."
    d)   End up with a mismatched partner who doesn't like to do things with me."
    e)   Be left for a younger woman when I'm too old to find another man."

DO NOT READ THE NEXT SECTION BEFORE TAKING THE QUIZ!

Scoring your Quiz

In this section, we will be converting your answers into number scores. You will then refer to the trait charts in the back of the book and to find the list of breeds that matches your scores for the different traits.

Energy Index

The first four traits we test for have to do with the amount of energy a woman needs, or can deal with, in a potential partner. These are Vitality (a scale that measures the man's range of physical vigor/gentleness), Indoor Activity, Outdoor Activity, and a trait we call "Need to Work".

Vitality - Question 1:
For an (a) answer, give yourself a score of 3.
For a (b) answer, give yourself a score of 2.
For a (c) answer, give yourself a score of 1

To score the next three traits…

Indoor Activity – Question 2
Outdoor Activity – Question 3

"Need to Work" – Question 4

Simply repeat the instructions for Question 1.

Once you've established your numbers for the four traits, turn to look at the Energy Index charts on pages 302-305. On a sheet of paper, jot down the breeds that appear in all four boxes. Beneath those breeds, jot down the breeds that appear in at least three of the boxes indicated by your scores. Then, continue to score the next four traits in the Intelligence Index.

Intelligence Index

The next four traits we test for have to do with the kind of mind a woman needs in her partner. These traits include Intelligence, Rate of Learning, the Ability to Cooperate, and level of Predictability in the man.

Intellect – Question 5
For an (a) answer, give yourself a score of 1.
For a (b) answer, give yourself a score of 2.
For a (c) answer, give yourself a score of 3.

Repeat these instructions for...
Learning Rate – Question 6
Cooperation – Question 8

Once you've found your number for these two traits, you'll score...

Predictability – Question 7

For an (a) answer, give yourself a score of 3.
For a (b) answer, give yourself a score of 2.
For a (c) answer, give yourself a score of 1.

After you've established your numbers for the four Intelligence Index traits, turn to the charts on pages 306-309. On your sheet of paper, jot down the breeds (if any) that appear in all four of the boxes that are indicated by your scores. Beneath those breeds, jot down breeds that appear in at least three of the boxes. Then, continue to score the next four traits in the Emotional Index.

Emotional Index

This section of the Quiz will establish the kind of partner a woman needs in order to have her emotional needs met. These traits include Emotional Openness, "Good with Kids", a scale of Extroversion, and Emotional Stability.

Emotional Openness – Question 9
Extroversion – Question 11

For an (a) answer, give yourself a score of 1.
For a (b) answer, give yourself a score of 2.
For a (c) answer, give yourself a score of 3.

"Good with Kids" – Question 10
Emotional Stability – Question 12

For an (a) answer, give yourself a score of 3.
For a (b) answer, give yourself a score of 2.
For a (c) answer, give yourself a score of 1.

Once you've established your numbers for the four traits, turn to look at the Intelligence Index charts on pages 298-301. On a sheet of paper, jot down the breeds (if any) that appear in all four boxes. Beneath those breeds, jot down the breeds that appear in at least three of the boxes indicated by your scores. Then, continue to score the next four traits in the Dominance Index.

Dominance Index

These questions are meant to establish levels of dominance behaviors the woman needs from or can tolerate in a man. These traits include Dominance (with men), Bossiness (with you or other family members), Territoriality, and Guarding Behavior.

Dominance – Question 13
Bossiness – Question 14
Territoriality - Question 15
Guarding Behavior – Question 16

For an (a) answer, give yourself a score of 1.
For a (b) answer, give yourself a score of 2.
For a (c) answer, give yourself a score of 3.

Once you've found your numbers for the four Dominance

Index traits, turn to the charts on pages 294-297 On your sheet of paper, jot down the breeds that appear in all four boxes.

Roaming

Question 17 deals with your tolerance for a tendency to "roam" in a mate.

For an (a) or a (b) answer, give yourself a score of 3.
For a (c) or (d) answer, give yourself a score of 2.
For an (e) of (f) answer, give yourself a score of 1.

Turn to the "Roaming" chart on page 311 to find your matching breeds for the Roaming question.

Adding it All Up

Look back over the breeds you've jotted down. Do any dogs appear in all the boxes indicated by your scores? Are there at least some dogs that appear in three of the boxes for each Index?

If you are a moderate person, looking for moderate levels of all these traits in a partner, you may have more possible matches than a person who has given more extreme or varied answers to the questions. You may even have several breeds that appear in every box indicated by your scores. Why does this happen? For the same reason there are more middle managers in the world than there are rich and powerful CEOs. Extremes of beauty, intelligence, willpower and athletic talent are rare.

If one or more of our "dogs" appears in all the boxes indicated by your scores: You've found your perfect match or several matching breeds that would suit you perfectly.

If one or more dogs appears in at least three of the boxes in each Index: You've found a suitable match, though you may have to give a little more to make it work. (You may also want to continue scoring the final two "weighted" questions, to establish whether Energy, Intelligence, Emotional, or Dominance traits are most important to match exactly.)

If your answers have been more extreme or varied and there is no dog that appears in all the boxes, or even in three of the boxes for each category: You should continue scoring our weighted questions below.

Weighted Question

Question 18 is different from the other questions in our Quiz. Scoring this question will tell you which areas of compatibility are most and least important to you.

Looking at the number value you've given to the (a) answer, the (b) answer, the (c) answer, the (d) answer, and the (e) answer. Which of these letters received your lowest rating? Which received your highest?

For those who found no single breed appearing in all matching trait boxes: If (a) received your highest score, the traits in the Dominance Index are most important to you. If (b) was highest, traits in the Intellectual Index are most important. Likewise, a high score in (c) corresponds to the Emotional Index. A high rating in (d) corresponds to the Energy Index.

To find the breed that is the best possible match, look at the breeds you jotted down for the Index that received your highest score. Do any dogs appear in all four Dominance trait boxes? If so, do any of those dogs appear in two or three indicated boxes for each of the other three Indexes? If this is the case, you've found your best possible match.

If (e) was your answer, it is important that your partner shares your ideas about roaming. Whichever of the breeds found in the corresponding "roaming" chart matches in the highest number of other categories would be your best match.

For those with no matching breeds, and few or no suitable breeds: If (a) received your lowest score, the traits in the Dominance Index are least important to you. If (b) was lowest, traits in the Intellectual Index are least important. Likewise, a low rating in (c) corresponds to the Emotional Index and a low rating in (d) corresponds to the Energy Index.

To find the breed that is the best possible match, you may completely disregard the boxes that fall within the Index that received your lowest score. Look at the matching boxes for the other three Indexes. Is there a breed that appears in all four of the trait boxes for each Index? Is there a breed that appears in three for each Index? If not, your matching dog is a Mixed Breed…

Mixed Breed Match

Face up to it. You're a high-maintenance and very picky woman and you need a very versatile man. You need a mixed breed and there's nothing wrong with that. My sister's husband is a very interesting Basenji/Brittany Spaniel mix.

To find your match, look through your matching boxes for each of the sixteen breed traits. Find the two breeds that appear the most, combine them and you've got your match. If there are more than three that appear the same number of times, choose two that appear in the two Indexes (Dominance, Intellectual, Emotional, or Energy) that received your two highest scores in the weighted questions.

About the Men's Quiz

Okay, boys... this one's for you! I realize that many of you will be taking this quiz at the prodding of an insistent female, so I'll try to make this as painless (and as much fun) as possible.

In case you're feeling a little "eeshy" about being compared to dogs, try and keep your eye on the prize. We're working in your best interest here. As a man, you know that women are always trying to change you, improve you, mold you to fit their impossible idea of a dream man. I know that this makes you crazy. And we both want the torture to end. For everyone. The result of this Quiz will tell your woman exactly what she can expect from you and what she must learn to live with... or without. (If you're honest, you'll have to confess that you're not always great about letting her know.) Trust me. This will make your life a whole lot easier.

By answering the Men's Quiz questions, and recording the answers on our Porch Dogs chart, you will be given a rating of 1-5 in each of 16 categories. Each category corresponds to a personality trait, like extroversion or energy level, found in both men and dogs. Your result will help you find your matching dog! If he's the same as one of your lady's matching breeds, you're a lucky man and your life together should be heaven on earth. If not, you've at least given her information about who you are and what your needs are. And if she still tries to change you? Remind her of that well-worn phrase... "You can't teach an old dog new tricks!"

Men's Quiz: A Matter of Breeding
(or... What kind of Dog am I?)

It's important to answer the questions as honestly as possible. If a question refers to your wife, and you don't have a wife, think about how you might feel if you had one, or substitute the word "girlfriend" in your mind. Same with kids. If you don't have any, just imagine that you do. And have fun!

1)   **Which Rock-N-Roll "oldie" title would your wife or girlfriend say best describes you in your relationship?**

    a)   Leader of the Pack
    b)   Johnny Angel
    c)   Cathy's Clown

2)   **Your girlfriend has just moved in with you. On the first day of the move, you come home to find that all your tapes, records and CD's have been mixed together on one shelf. How does that make you feel?**

    a)   Angry. She knows I don't like anyone messing with my stuff.
    b)   Slightly annoyed. I had everything organized so I could find it.
    c)   Fine. That's what living together is all about.

3) **The very attractive girl you're dating tells you she's going to start jogging in the park at night after work. Your response is...**

a) "No. You're not."

b) "You know, I've been thinking of jogging after work too. Maybe we should jog together."

c) "You should really consider getting some friends to go with you. The park can be dangerous at night."

4) **You're on a date in a restaurant when a waitress comes to your table with a drink for your date. "It's from the gentleman in the corner" she says, and points out the smiling stranger. What's your first reaction?**

a) I'll invite him outside for a private chat about manners and the cost of dental implants.

b) I drink the drink myself, turn, and wink at the guy.

c) She's a grown woman, I'm sure she'll decide what she needs to do.

5) **Which of the following sports would your wife or girlfriend say best describes your sex life?**

    a)   Rugby: a real free-for-all – lots of energy, almost no rules.

    b)   Basketball: a team effort - a lot of passing off and physical under the boards.

    c)   Pairs figure skating: with skill and imagination, you lift your partner to new heights of pleasure.

6) **Imagine you and your wife or girlfriend are stuck inside together over a rainy weekend. By Sunday evening, which of the following cartoon characters would she say is most like you, as far as sheer physical energy is concerned?**

    a) The Road Runner

    b) Pepe Le Pew

    c) Droopy Dog

7) **Your significant other has just asked you to get the yard ready for a barbecue she's planned with some friends. Your first thought is...**

   a) I hate her mower. I'll run home and get my riding mower... and my trimmer and my chain saw.

   b) No problem. I'd rather be working outside than running errands.

   c) If we leave the weeds and put up a tiki torch, it'll look like a jungle theme.

8) **Your woman has started complaining (well, nagging really) about the amount of time you spend at work. You come back with...**

   a) My work is my passion. Always has been, always will be.

   b) I work so we can have the things we want.

   c) If you can support us, I'd honestly love to quit.

9) **Things have been a bit strained at home lately. Your wife or girlfriend tells you she wants the two of you to see a relationship counselor. Your response is...**

   a) Great. Maybe we can get to the bottom of our problems.

   b) Why don't we try to work things out at home, before we ask for outside help?

   c) I'd rather have my ass waxed.

10) **Your dream girl tells you that she envisions her life with a lot of children and can't imagine marrying a man who doesn't feel the same way. Your first reaction is...**

    a)   Wow! She really is my dream girl.

    b)   "A lot" is such a relative term. I'm sure we can compromise.

    c)   She's kidding, right? Oh, God, I hope she's kidding.

11) **Your idea of the perfect party is ...**

    a)   A room packed with high energy people, a great band and my own personal spotlight.

    b)   Some old friends, some new faces and a few odd-balls to keep it interesting.

    c)   A few close friends, good food and great conversation.

12) **Think about your old high school or college pals. Which statement best describes your place in the group?**

    a)   I was the calm stable guy who tried to keep the others out of trouble.

    b)   I was the clown of the group, a prankster.

    c)   The guy who'd do anything on a dare. I was the cause of most of the trouble we got into

13) **Your buddy has asked you to be one of his "phone-a-friends" on the Who Wants To Be A Millionaire TV show. You are his expert for which category?**

    a)   Almost any category. I'm a human encyclopedia.

    b)   Books and movies, music and entertainment trivia.

    c)   Sports stats and brands of beer.

14) **Imagine you've been a bachelor for the past five years. Suddenly you find yourself in a relationship with a woman who tells you it's very important to her that you always put the toilet seat down. How long will it take you to remember to do it?**

    a)   It's important to her? It'll take a week or two, tops.

    b)   Months. I'll try to remember, but old habits die hard.

    c)   I'll always screw up once in a while. You can't teach on old dog new tricks.

15) **Your wife has wanted to take ballroom dancing classes for years, but the only class available is on the night of your regular poker game. What would she have to do to get you to go to the class with her?**

    a)   Just ask.

    b)   Promise me hot sex after each class.

    c)   Move the game to the dancehall, then dance around us while we play poker.

16) **What is your attitude toward change?**

    a)   I thrive on change. It keeps life interesting.

    b)   A little change never hurt anybody.

    c)   Why change when I'm this close to perfection?

17) **Your boss sends you to a conference out of town where you meet an incredibly sexy woman who lets you know she's willing. Though you're happily married you...**

    a)   Go for it! What she doesn't know won't hurt her.

    b)   Tell myself that it doesn't count as cheating because I'm out of town.

    c)   It couldn't hurt just to have a few drinks and some mild flirtation, could it?

    d)   Do everything but "the deed" and torture myself for years to come.

    e)   Turn her down flat. I would never cheat on my wife.

    f)   Miss all the signals and never even know the woman was interested.

18) **Considering mainly your physical build, if you were cast in a war movie, which part would they hire you to play?**

a) "Bruiser" - the tough guy – all muscle, all man.

b) "Big Ben" – big but gentle, dies saving his pals.

c) "Golden Boy" – the All-American guy next door.

d) "Slim" – the intelligence officer, lean, quick and agile.

e) "Dealer" – the con artist, a little guy, but tough and wiry.

f) "Shakespeare" – sensitive, dies as soon as the first shots are fired.

19) **If you could be present at your own wake, which toast would you be most likely to hear?**

a) No man would cross him, no man could boss him, but most men would buy him a drink.

b) His was an original mind... maybe a little too original.

c) So many people loved this guy, there's a scalper outside selling tickets to his wake.

d) Some say he lived life on the edge. All I know is, when I looked up the word "Extreme" in the dictionary, his picture was there.

e) Wherever he went, he left a trail of moist panties and broken hearts.

DO NOT READ THE NEXT SECTION BEFORE TAKING THE QUIZ!

Scoring Your Quiz

By far the easiest way to score the quiz is by visiting the Porch Dogs web site - **www.porchdogs.com** - and entering your answers on the site's electronic version of the quiz, which will give you an instant match.

Or, if your wife, girlfriend, daughter, or sister forced you to take this quiz, you are well within your rights to hand it to her and tell her to score it.

If you're scoring your own quiz, we'll begin by scoring the four traits in the Dominance Index.

Dominance Index

The first four traits we test for have to do with your need to be in control of certain situations. These traits include Dominance (with other men), Bossiness (or dominance within your relationship/family), Territoriality, and Guarding Behavior.

Bossiness – Question 1

For an (a) answer, give yourself a score of 3.
For a (b) answer, give yourself a score of 2.
For a (c) answer, give yourself a score of 1.

To score the next three traits, simply repeat these instructions for...

Territoriality – Question 2
Guarding Behavior – Question 3
Dominance – Question 4

Once you've established numbers for the four traits, turn to look at the Dominance Index charts on pages 294-297. On a sheet of paper, jot down any breeds that appear in all four of the boxes that correspond with your numbers for each trait. Beneath those breeds, jot down breeds that appear in at least three of the boxes. Then continue to score the nest four traits in the Energy Index.

Energy Index

These four traits have to do with the amount of energy you give to different kinds of activities. These are Vitality (which measures your range of physical vigor versus gentleness), Indoor Activity, Outdoor Activity, and Roaming (sexual energy, willingness to stray).

Vitality – Question 5
Indoor Activity – Question 6
Outdoor Activity – Question 7
"Need to Work" – Question 8

For an (a) answer, give yourself a score of 3.
For a (b) answer, give yourself a score of 2.
For a (c) answer, give yourself a score of 1.

Once you've established your numbers for the four Energy traits, turn to the Energy Index charts on pages 302-305. On your sheet of paper, jot down the breeds that appear in all four of the corresponding boxes. Beneath those breeds, jot down breeds that appear in at least three of the boxes indicated by your scores. Then, continue to score the next four traits in the Emotional Index.

Emotional Index

This section of the Quiz will establish your levels in four emotional traits. These traits include Emotional Openness (within your relationship or with family), a trait we call "Good with Kids", a scale of Extroversion (or openness with strangers), and Emotional Stability.

Openness – Question 9
"Good with Kids" – Question 10
Emotional Stability – Question 12

For an (a) answer, give yourself a score of 3.
For a (b) answer, give yourself a score of 2.
For a (c) answer, give yourself a score of 1.

Extroversion – Question 11

For an (a) answer, give yourself a score of 1
For a (b) answer, give yourself a score of 2.
For a (c) answer, give yourself a score of 3.

Turn to the Emotional Index charts on pages 298-301. On your sheet of paper, jot down the breeds (if any) that appear in all four of the appropriate trait boxes. Beneath those breeds, jot down the breeds that appear in any three of the boxes. Then continue to score the next four traits in the Intelligence Index.

Intelligence Index

The next four traits we test for have to do with the way your mind works. These traits include Intellect (as in IQ), Learning Rate (how long it takes to learn new material), Cooperation (or learning to give up some of your own ideas to better coexist with a partner), and your level of Predictability (how likely you are to repeat behavior patterns).

Intellect – Question 13
Cooperation – Question 15
For an (a) answer, give yourself a score of 3.

For a (b) answer, give yourself a score of 2.
For a (c) answer, give yourself a score of 1.

Learning Rate – Question 14
Predictability – Question 16

For an (a) answer, give yourself a score of 1.
For a (b) answer, give yourself a score of 2.
For a (c) answer, give yourself a score of 3.

Once you've established your levels for the four Intelligence Index traits, turn to the charts on pages 306-309. On your sheet of paper, jot down the breeds that appear in all four of the level boxes indicated by your scores. Beneath those breeds, jot down any that appear in at least three of the boxes. Then continue to score the last two traits.

Roaming - Question 17

For an (a) or a (b) answer, give yourself a score of 3.
For a (c) or (d) answer, give yourself a score of 2.
For an (e) of (f) answer, give yourself a score of 1.
Turn to the "Roaming" chart on page 311 to find your matching breeds for the Roaming question.

Size and Build

Now, look at question 18. This question is designed to tell us something about your physical self.

For each (a) answer, give yourself a score of 6.
For each (b) answer, give yourself a score of 5.
For each (c) answer, give yourself a score of 4.
For each (d) answer, give yourself a score of 3.
For each (e) answer, give yourself a score of 2.
For each (f) answer, give yourself a score of 1.

Turn to the chart on page 310, to find your matching breeds.

The Weighted Question

Question 19 tells you which trait you judge yourself by, which is the trait most important to match. If you picked **(a)**, you consider yourself to be a dominant male. If you picked **(b)**, your intelligence is most important to you. Likewise **(c)** for extroversion and **(d)** for outdoor energy. And if you chose **(e)**, you consider yourself to be quite a ladies man and are therefore more likely to roam.

Adding it All Up

Look back over the breeds you've jotted down. Does any dog appear in all the boxes indicated by your scores? If so, this is your matching breed.

If more than one dog appears in every box: You must read the entry for each separate dog and decide which one is your best match. To help you decide, look at your answer to Question 19, the weighted question.

If no dog appears in every box indicated by your scores: You must begin to look at the dogs who appear in at least three trait boxes for each Index, making sure to match the trait you chose in the weighted question (#19). Jot down the dogs that appear in the most boxes. The dog listed in the greatest number of matching boxes is your breed.

If your answers have been so extreme or varied that no dogs appear in at least three boxes in each Index, you are a mixed breed: Find the two dogs that appear in the greatest number of boxes. You are a mix between these two breeds. Your perfect partner will be a match with both of these dogs. A suitable partner will match at least one of them.

Trait Charts

1

Beagle, Bichon Frise, Brittany Spaniel, Cavalier King Charles Spaniel, Chihuahua, Cocker Spaniel, Collie, English Setter, Foxhound, Golden Retriever, Harrier, Irish Setter, Italian Greyhound, Japanese Chin, Keeshond, Maltese, Papillon, Pharaoh Hound, Pug, Shetland Sheepdog, Silky, Springer Spaniel, Toy Poodle, Whippet

2

Australian Shepherd, Basset Hound, Bernese Mountain Dog, Bloodhound, Border Tr, Borzoi, Boston Tr, Boxer, Briard, Brussels Griffon, Cairn Tr, Chesapeake Bay Retriever, Dachshund, Dalmatian, German Pointer, Great Dane, Great Pyrenees, Irish Wolfhound, Labrador Retriever, Lhasa Apso, Newfoundland, Norwich Tr, Old English Sheepdog, Pekingese, Pointer, Poodle, Porch Dog, Saint Bernard, Saluki, Samoyed, Schipperke, Scottish Deerhound, Siberian Husky, Soft-Coated Wheaten Tr, Tibetan Tr, Vizsla, Welsh Corgi, West Highland White Tr, Wirehaired Pointing Griffon

3

Airedale, Afghan Hound, Akita, Alaskan Malamute, American Pit Bull or Staffordshire Tr, Australian Cattle Dog, Basenji, Belgians, Black and Tan Coonhound, Border Collie, Bouvier des Flandres, Bulldog, Bullmastiff, Bull Tr, Chow Chow, Doberman Pinscher, Fox Tr, German Shepherd, Giant Schnauzer, Gordon Setter, Jack Russell Tr, Komondor, Miniature Pinscher, Norwegian Elkhound, Pomeranian, Puli, Rhodesian Ridgeback, Rottweiler, Scottish Tr, ShihTzu, Standard Schnauzer, Weimaraner, Yorkshire Tr

Dominance Index - Bossiness

1

Afghan Hound, Basset Hound, Beagle, Bernese Mountain Dog, Bichon Frise, Border Tr, Boston Tr, Boxer, Cavalier King Charles Spaniel, Cocker Spaniel, English Setter, Foxhound, Golden Retriever, Harrier, Irish Setter, Italian Greyhound, Japanese Chin, Keeshond, Maltese, Newfoundland, Old English Sheepdog, Papillon, Pharaoh Hound, Pug, Saluki, Samoyed, Scottish Deerhound, Shetland Sheepdog, Silky, Springer Spaniel, Tibetan Tr, Toy Poodle, Vizsla, Whippet, Wirehaired Pointing Griffon

2

Airedale, Alaskan Malamute, Australian Shepherd, Basenji, Basset Hound, Belgians, Black and Tan Coonhound, Bloodhound, Borzoi, Boxer, Brittany Spaniel, Bulldog, Cairn Tr, Chesapeake Bay Retriever, Collie, Dachshund, Dalmatian, Fox Tr, German Pointer, German Shepherd, Gordon Setter, Great Dane, Great Pyrenees, Irish Wolfhound, Labrador Retriever, Lhasa Apso, Norwich Tr, Pointer, Poodle, Porch Dog, Saint Bernard, Schipperke, Siberian Husky, Soft-coated Wheaten Tr, West Highland White Tr, Yorkshire Tr

3

Akita, American Pit Bull or Staffordshire Tr, Australian Cattle Dog, Border Collie, Briard, Brussels Griffon, Bouvier des Flandres, Bullmastiff, Bull Tr, Chihuahua, Chow Chow, Doberman Pinscher, Giant Schnauzer, Jack Russell Tr, Komondor, Miniature Pinscher, Norwegian Elkhound, Pekingese, Puli, Rhodesian Ridgeback, Rottweiler, Scottish Tr, ShihTzu, Standard Schnauzer, Weimaraner, Welsh Corgi

Dominance Index - Territoriality

1

Basset Hound, Beagle, Bichon Frise, Border Tr, Borzoi, Boston Tr, Cavalier King Charles Spaniel, Cocker Spaniel, Collie, English Setter, Foxhound, German Pointer, Golden Retriever, Harrier, Irish Setter, Italian Greyhound, Japanese Chin, Keeshond, Newfoundland, Papillon, Pharaoh Hound, Pointer, Saint Bernard, Saluki, Scottish Deerhound, Siberian Husky, ShihTzu, Silky, Soft-Coated Wheaten Tr, Springer Spaniel, Toy Poodle, Vizsla, West Highland White Tr, Whippet

2

Airedale, Afghan Hound, Belgians, Bernese Mountain Dog, Black and Tan Coonhound, Bloodhound, Border Collie, Bouvier des Flandres, Boxer, Brittany Spaniel, Brussels Griffon, Cairn Tr, Dachshund, Dalmatian, Labrador Retriever, Gordon Setter, Great Dane, Great Pyrenees, Irish Wolfhound, Lhasa Apso, Maltese, Norwich Tr, Old English Sheepdog, Pekingese, Pomeranian, Poodle, Porch Dog, Pug, Samoyed, Shetland Sheepdog, Tibetan Tr, Welsh Corgi, Wirehaired Pointing Griffon

3

Akita, Alaskan Malamute, American Pit Bull or Staffordshire Tr, Australian Cattle Dog, Australian Shepherd, Basenji, Briard, Bulldog, Bullmastiff, Bull Tr, Chesapeake Bay Retriever, Chihuahua, Chow Chow, Doberman Pinscher, Fox Tr, German Shepherd, Giant Schnauzer, Jack Russell Tr, Komondor, Miniature Pinscher, Norwegian Elkhound, Puli, Rhodesian Ridgeback, Rottweiler, Schipperke Scottish Tr, Standard Schnauzer, Weimaraner, Yorkshire Tr

Dominance Index - Guarding Behavior

1   Afghan Hound, Basset Hound, Beagle, Bichon Frise, Border Tr, Borzoi, Boston Tr, Brittany Spaniel, Brussels Griffon, Cavalier King Charles Spaniel, Cairn Tr, Chihuahua, Cocker Spaniel, Dachshund, English Setter, Foxhound, Fox Tr, Golden Retriever, Harrier, Irish Setter, Italian Greyhound, Japanese Chin, Keeshond, Maltese, Miniature Pinscher, Norwich Tr, Papillon, Pekingese, Pug, Saint Bernard, Saluki, Samoyed, Scottish Deerhound, Scottish Tr, Shetland Sheepdog, ShihTzu, Silky, Springer Spaniel, Toy Poodle, Vizsla, West Highland White Tr, Whippet, Yorkshire Tr

2   Alaskan Malamute, Australian Cattle Dog, Australian Shepherd, Basenji, Bloodhound, Border Collie, Bull Tr, Collie, Dalmation, Gordon Setter, Great Dane, Irish Wolfhound, Jack Russell Tr, Labrador Retriever, Lhasa Apso, Newfoundland, Norwegian Elkhound, Old English Sheepdog, Pharaoh Hound, Pointer, Poodle, Porch Dog, Siberian Husky, Soft-Coated Wheaten Tr, Springer Spaniel, Tibetan Tr, Wirehaired Pointing Griffon

3   Airedale, Akita, American Pit Bull or Staffordshire Tr, Belgians, Bernese Mountain Dog, Black and Tan Coonhound, Boxer, , Bouvier des Flandres, Briard, Bulldog, Bullmastiff, Chesapeake Bay Retriever, Chow Chow, Doberman Pinscher, German Pointer, German Shepherd, Giant Schnauzer, Great Pyrenees, Komondor, Puli, Rhodesian Ridgeback, Rottweiler, Schipperke, Standard Schnauzer, Weimaraner, Welsh Corgi

1

Afghan Hound, American Pit Bull or Staffordshire Tr, Belgians, Borzoi, Chihuahua, Chow Chow, Dachshund, Giant Schnauzer, Komondor, Miniature Pinscher, Norwich Tr, Pekingese, Pharoah Hound, Pomeranian, Puli, Rottweiler, Rhodesian Ridgeback, Saluki, Schipperke, Scottish Tr, Standard Schnauzer, Toy Poodle, Tibetan Tr, Whippet, Wirehaired Pointing Griffon

2

Airedale, Akita, Australian Shepherd, Basenji, Bernese Mountain Dog, Black and Tan Coonhound, Border Tr, Boston Tr, Bouvier des Flandres, Briard, Bullmastiff, Bull Tr, Cairn Tr, Collie, Chesapeake Bay Retriever, Dalmatian, Doberman Pinscher, German Pointer, German Shepherd, Great Pyrenees, Harrier, Irish Wolfhound, Italian Greyhound, Labrador Retriever, Lhasa Apso, Maltese, Pointer, Poodle, Porch Dog, Pug, Saint Bernard, Samoyed, Shetland Sheepdog, Silky, Weimaraner, Yorkshire Tr

3

Alaskan Malamute, Australian Cattle Dog, Basset Hound, Beagle, Bichon Frise, Bloodhound, Border Collie, Boxer, Brittany Spaniel, Brussels Griffon, Bulldog, Cavalier King Charles Spaniel, Cocker Spaniel, English Setter, Foxhound, Fox Tr, Golden Retriever, Gordon Setter, Great Dane, Irish Setter, Jack Russell Tr, Japanese Chin, Keeshond, Newfoundland, Norwegian Elkhound, Old English Sheepdog, Papillon, Scottish Deerhound, Shih Tzu, Siberian Husky, Soft-Coated Wheaten Tr, , Springer Spaniel, Vizsla, Welsh Corgi, West Highland White Tr

Emotional Index -"Good with Kids"

1

Afghan Hound, Airedale, Akita, American Pit Bull or Staffordshire Tr, Basenji, Border Collie, Borzoi, Bull Tr, Cairn Tr, Chihuahua, Chow Chow, Dachshund, Dalmatian, Doberman Pinscher, German Pointer, Giant Schnauzer, Great Pyrenees, Itallian Greyhound, Jack Russell Tr, Komondor, Lhasa Apso, Maltese, Miniature Pinscher, Norwegian Elkhound, Pekingese, Pomeranian, Puli, Rhodesian Ridgeback, Rottweiler Saluki, Schipperke, Scottish Tr, Standard Schnauzer, Tibetan Tr, Toy Poodle, Whippet, Wirehaired Pointing Griffon

2

Alaskan Malamute, Australian Cattle Dog, Australian Shepherd, Beagle, Belgians, Black and Tan Coonhound, Border Tr, Boston Tr, Bouvier des Flandres, Boxer, Briard, Brussels Griffon, Bullmastiff, Chesapeake Bay Retriever, Fox Tr, Great Dane, Japanese Chin, Norwegian Elkhound, Norwich Tr, Papillon, Pointer, Shetland Sheepdog, Shih Tzu, Silky, Vizsla, Weimaraner, Welsh Corgi, West Highland White Tr, Yorkshire Tr

3

Basset Hound, Beagle, Bernese Mountain Dog, Bichon Frise, Bloodhound, Brittany Spaniel, Bulldog, Cavalier King Charles Spaniel, Cocker Spaniel, Collie, English Setter, Foxhound, German Shepherd, Golden Retriever, Gordon Setter, Harrier, Irish Setter, Irish Wolfhound, Keeshond, Labrador Retriever, Newfoundland, Old English Sheepdog, Pharoah Hound, Poodle, Porch Dog, Pug, Saint Bernard, Samoyed, Scottish Deerhound, Siberian Husky, Soft-Coated Wheaten Tr, Springer Spaniel

Emotional Index - Extroversion

1

Afghan Hound, Akita, Belgians, Bernese Mountain Dog, Borzoi, Boxer, Briard, Bullmastiff, Bull Tr, Chesapeake Bay Retriever, Chihuahua, Chow Chow, Dachshund, Dalmatian, Doberman Pinscher, Giant Schnauzer, Italian Greyhound, Komondor, Lhasa Apso, Maltese, Miniature Pinscher, Pekingese, Pomeranian, Pug, Puli, Rhodesian Ridgeback, Rottweiler, Saluki, Samoyed, Schipperke, Scottish Tr, Standard Schnauzer, Tibetan Tr, Toy Poodle, Weimaraner, Whippet

2

Airedale, American Pit Bull or Staffordshire Tr, Australian Cattle Dog, Australian Shepherd, Basset Hound, Black and Tan Coonhound, Border Tr, Boston Tr, Bouvier Des Flandres, Brussels Griffon, Bulldog, Cairn Tr, Collie, Fox Tr, German Pointer, German Shepherd, Gordon Setter, Harrier, Irish Wolfhound, Jack Russell Tr, Norwegian Elkhound, Norwich Tr, Pharoah Hound, Pointer, Poodle, Shetland Sheepdog,Shih Tzu, Silky, Springer Spaniel, Welsh Corgi, Wirehaired Pointing Griffon, Yorkshire Tr

3

Alaskan Malamute, Basenji, Beagle, Bichon Frise, Bloodhound, Border Collie, Brittany Spaniel, Cavalier King Charles Spaniel, Cocker Spaniel, English Setter, Foxhound, Golden Retriever, Great Dane, Great Pyrenees, Irish Setter, Japanese Chin, Keeshond, Labrador Retriever, Newfoundland, Old English Sheepdog, Papillon, Porch Dog, Saint Bernard, Scottish Deerhound, Siberian Husky, Soft-Coated Wheaten Tr, Vizsla, West Highland White Tr

1

Belgians, Border Collie, Borzoi, Boston Tr, Brittany Spaniel, Brussels Griffon, Chihuahua, Cocker Spaniel, Dachshund, Dalmatian, Doberman Pinscher, Irish Setter, Italian Greyhound, Lhasa Apso, Miniature Pinscher, Papillon, Puli, Saluki, Schipperke, Shetland Sheepdog, Tibetan Tr, Toy Poodle, Vizsla, West Highland White Tr, Whippet, Wirehaired Pointing Griffon, Yorkshire Tr

2

Afghan Hound, American Pit Bull or Staffordshire, Australian Cattle Dog, Australian Shepherd, Basenji, Basset Hound, Beagle, Bouvier des Flandres, Briard, Cairn Tr, Collie, Foxhound, German Pointer, German Shepherd, Gordon Setter, Jack Russell Tr, Komondor, Maltese, Old English Sheepdog, Pekingese, Pharoah Hound, Pointer, Pomeranian, Poodle, Porch Dog, Rottweiler, Samoyed, Springer Spaniel, Welsh Corgi, Weimaraner

3

Airedale, Akita, Alaskan Malamute, Basset Hound, Bernese Mountain Dog, Bichon Frise, Black and Tan Coonhound, Bloodhound, Border Tr, Boxer, Bulldog, Bullmastiff, Bull Tr, Cavalier King Charles Spaniel, Chesapeake Bay Retriever, Chow Chow, English Setter, Fox Tr, Giant Schnauzer, Golden Retriever, Great Dane, Great Pyrenees, Harrier, Irish Wolfhound, Japanese Chin, Keeshond, Labrador Retriever, Newfoundland, Norwegian Elkhound, Norwich Tr, Pug, Rhodesian Ridgeback, Saint Bernard, Scottish Deerhound, Scottish Tr, Shih Tzu, Siberian Husky, Silky, Soft-coated Wheaten Tr, Shi Tzu, Standard Schnauzer

Energy Index - Vitality

1

Afghan Hound, Basenji, Beagle, Belgians, Bernese Mountain Dog, Bichon Frise, Border Terrier, Boston Tr, Borzoi, Bouvier des Flandres, Bulldog, Cavalier King Charles Spaniel, Chihuahua, Cocker Spaniel, Collie, Great Dane, Irish Wolfhound, Italian Greyhound, Japanese Chin, Keeshond, Maltese, Newfoundland, Old English Sheepdog, Papillon, Pug, Saint Bernard, Saluki, Scottish Deerhound, Shetland Sheepdog, Toy Poodle, Whippet

2

Australian Cattle Dog, Australian Shepherd, Basset Hound, Border Collie, Brussels Griffon, Cairn Tr, Chesapeake Bay Retriever, English Setter, Golden Retriever, Labrador Retriever, Miniature Pinscher, Norwich Tr, Pekingese, Pharoah Hound, Pomeranian, Poodle, Porch Dog, Samoyed, Scottish Tr, Silky, Shih Tzu, Siberian Husky, Springer Spaniel, Welsh Corgi, West Highland White Tr, Yorkshire Tr

3

Airedale, Akita, Alaskan Malamute, American Pit Bull or Staffordshire, Black and Tan Coonhound, Bloodhound, Boxer, Brittany Spaniel, Briard, Bullmastiff, Bull Tr, Chow Chow. Dachshund, Dalmatian, Doberman Pinscher, Foxhound, Fox Tr, German Pointer, German Shepherd, Giant Schnauzer, Gordon Setter, Great Pyrenees, Harrier, Irish Setter, Jack Russell Tr, Komondor, Lhasa Apso, Norwegian Elkhound, Pointer, Puli, Rhodesian Ridgeback, Rottweiler, Schipperke, Soft-Coated Wheaten Tr, Standard Schnauzer, Tibetan Tr, Vizsla, Weimaraner, Wirehaired Pointing Griffon

Energy Index - Indoor Activity

1
Afghan Hound, Akita, Basset Hound, Bernese Mountain Dog, Black and Tan Coonhound, Bloodhound, Borzoi, Boston Tr, Bouvier des Flandres, Bulldog, Bullmastiff, Cavalier King Charles Spaniel, Chesapeake Bay Retriever, Chow Chow, Cocker Spaniel, Collie, English Setter, Great Dane, Great Pyrenees, Irish Wolfhound, Newfoundland, Pekingese, Pharoah Hound, Pug, Rhodesian Ridgeback, Rottweiler, Saint Bernard, Saluki, Scottish Deerhound, Whippet,

2
Australian Shepherd, Belgians, Border Tr, Boxer, Brittany Spaniel, Bull Tr, German Shepherd, Giant Schnauzer, Golden Retriever, Gordon Setter, Japanese Chin, Keeshond, Labrador Retriever, Norwegian Elkhound, Old English Sheepdog, Papillon, Poodle, Porch Dog, Shetland Sheepdog, Shih Tzu, Silky, Soft-Coated Wheaten Tr, Springer Spaniel, Tibetan Tr, Vizsla

3
Airedale, Alaskan Malamute, American Pit Bull or Staffordshire Tr, Australian Cattle Dog, Basenji, Beagle, Bichon Frise, Border Collie, Briard, Brussels Griffon, Cairn Tr, Chihuahua, Dachshund, Dalmatian, Doberman Pinscher, Foxhound, Fox Tr, German Pointer, Harrier, Irish Setter, Jack Russell Tr, Komondor, Lhasa Apso, Maltese, Miniature Pinscher, Norwich Tr, Pointer, Pomeranian, Puli, Samoyed, Schipperke, Scottish Tr, Siberian Husky, Standard Schnauzer, Toy Poodle, Weimaraner, Welsh Corgi, West Highland White Tr, Wirehaired Pointing Griffon, Yorkshire Terrier

Energy Index - Outdoor Activity

1 Basset Hound, Beagle, Bichon Frise, Boston Tr, Bulldog, Cairn Tr, Cocker Spaniel, Golden Retriever, Great Dane, Great Pyrenees, Irish Wolfhound, Japanese Chin, Lhasa Apso, Maltese, Norwegian Elkhound, Papillon, Pekingese, Pomeranian, Porch Dog, Pug, Saint Bernard, Shih Tzu, Tibetan Tr

2 American Pit Bull or Staffordshire Tr, Basenji, Belgians, Bernese Mountain Dog, Black and Tan Coonhound, Bloodhound, Border Tr, Bouvier des Flandres, Boxer, Bullmastiff, Bull Tr, Cavalier King Charles Spaniel, Chow Chow, Collie, German Shepherd, Giant Schnauzer, Keeshond, Labrador Retriever, Newfoundland, Poodle, Rottweiler, Scottish Deerhound, Soft-Coated Wheaten Tr, Silky, Vizsla, Welsh Corgi, Wirehaired Pointing Griffon

3 Afghan Hound, Airedale, Akita, Alaskan Malamute, Australian Cattle Dog. Australian Shepherd, Border Collie, Borzoi, Briard, Brittany Spaniel, Brussels Griffon, Chesapeake Bay Retriever, Chihauhua, Dachshund, Dalmation, Doberman Pinscher, English Setter, Foxhound, Fox Tr, German Pointer, Gordon Setter, Harrier, Irish Setter, Italian Greyhound, Jack Russell Tr, Komondor, Miniature Pinscher, Norwich Tr, Old English Sheepdog, Pharoah Hound, Pointer, Puli, Rhodesian Ridgeback, Saluki, Samoyed, Schipperke, Scottish Tr, Shetland Sheepdog, Siberian Husky, Springer Spaniel, Standard Schnauzer, Toy Poodle, Weimaraner, West Highland White Tr, Whippet, Yorkshire Tr

Energy Index - "Need to Work"

1

Afghan Hound, Basenji, Basset Hound, Beagle, Bichon Frise, Bloodhound, Borzoi, Boston Tr, Brussels Griffon, Bulldog, Cavalier King Charles Spaniel, Chihuahua, Chow Chow, Cocker Spaniel, Dachshund, Dalmatian, Golden Retriever, Irish Wolfhound, Italian Greyhound, Japenese Chin, Lhasa Apso, Maltese, Miniature Pinscher, Papillon, Pekingese, Pomeranian, Pug, Rhodesian Ridgeback, Schipperke, Shih Tzu, Silky, Tibetan Tr, Toy Poodle, Whippet, Yorkshire Tr

2

American Pit Bull or Staffordshire Tr, Bernese Mountain Dog, Black and Tan Coonhound, Boxer, Brittany Spaniel, Briard, Bullmastiff, Chesapeake Bay Retriever, Doberman Pinscher, English Setter, Foxhound, Golden Retriever, Gordon Setter, Great Dane, Harrier, Irish Setter, Keeshond, Komondor, Labrador Retriever, Old English Sheepdog, Pharoah Hound, Pointer, Poodle, Porch Dog, Saint Bernard, Saluki, Scottish Deerhound, Springer Spaniel, Wirehaired Pointing Griffon

3

Airdale, Akita, Alaskan Malamute, Australian Cattle Dog, Australian Shepherd, Belgian, Border Collie, Border Tr, Bouvier des Flandres, Cairn Tr, Collie, Fox Tr, German Pointer, German Shepherd, Giant Schnauzer, Great Pyrenees, Jack Russell Tr, Newfoundland, Norwegian Elkhound, Puli, Rottweiler, Samoyed, Scottish Tr, Shetland Sheepdog, Siberian Husky, Soft-Coated Wheaten Tr, Standard Schnauzer, Vizsla, Weimaraner, Welsh Corgi, West Highland White Tr

1
Akita, American Pit Bull or Staffordshire Tr, Basset Hound, Black and Tan Coonhound, Borzoi, Boston Tr, Boxer, Briard, Bulldog, Bullmastif, Bull Tr, Chesapeake Bay Retriever, Foxhound, Great Dane, Golden Retriever, Gordon Setter, Italian Greyhound, Keeshond, Komondor, Labrador Retriever, Lhasa Apso, Pekingese, Pointer, Pug, Rottweiler, Saluki, Scottish Deerhound, Scottish Tr, Shih Tzu, Springer Spaniel, Tibetan Tr, Vizsla, Whippet, Wirehaired Pointing Griffon

2
Afghan Hound, Airedale, Beagle, Belgians, Bernese Mountain Dog, Bloodhound, Border Tr, Bouvier des Flandres, Brittany Spaniel, Cavalier King Charles Spaniel, Chow Chow, Cocker Spaniel, Collie, Dalmatian, English Setter, German Pointer, Great Pyrenees, Harrier, Irish Setter, Irish Wolfhound, Keeshond, Maltese, Miniature Pinscher, Newfoundland, Norwich Tr, Old English Sheepdog, Papillon, Pomeranian, Porch Dog, Rhodesian Ridgeback, Saint Bernard, Silky, Soft-Coated Wheaten Tr, Weimaraner

3
Alaskan Malamute, Australian Cattle Dog, Australian Shepherd, Basenji, Bichon Frise, Border Collie, Brittany Spaniel, Brussels Griffon, Cairn Tr, Chihuahua, Dachsund, Doberman Pinscher, Fox Tr, German Shepherd, Giant Schnauzer, Jack Russell Tr, Japanese Chin, Norwegian Elkhound, Pharoah Hound, Poodle, Porch Dog, Puli, Samoyed, Schipperke, Shetland Sheepdog, Siberian Husky, Standard Schnauzer, Toy Poodle, Welsh Corgi, West Highland White Tr, Yorkshire tr

Intelligence Index - Rate of Learning

1

Afghan Hound, Alaskan Malamute, Basset Hound, Black and Tan Coonhound, Bloodhound, Boston Tr, Briard, Bulldog, Bull Tr, Chesapeake Bay Retriever, Dalmatian, English Setter, Fox Hound, Great Dane, Great Pyrenees, Komondor, Old English Sheepdog, Pointer, Porch Dog, Rottweiler, Saluki, Scottish Deerhound, Tibetan Tr

2

Airedale, Akita, American Pit Bull or Staffordshire Tr, Border Tr, Boxer, Brussels Griffon, Bullmastiff, Cairn Tr, Chihuahua, Chow Chow, Collie, Fox Tr, Giant Schnauzer, Irish Setter, Italian Greyhound, Japanese Chin, Keeshond, Lhasa Apso, Maltese, Miniature Pinscher, Newfoundland, Norwich Tr, Papillon, Pekingese, Pomeranian, Pug, Rhodesian Ridgeback, Saint Bernard, Samoyed, Schipperke, Scottish Tr, Shih Tzu, Siberian Husky, Silky, Soft-Coated Wheaten Tr, West Highland White Tr, Whippet

3

Australian Cattle Dog, Australian Shepherd, Basenji, Beagle, Belgians, Bernese Mountain Dog, Bichon Frise, Border Collie, Borzoi, Bouvier, Brittany Spaniel, Cavalier King Charles Spaniel, Cocker Spaniel, Dachshund, Doberman Pinscher, German Pointer, German Shepherd, Golden Retriever, Gordon Setter, Harrier, Irish Wolfhound, Jack Russell Tr, Keeshond, Labrador Retriever, Norwegian Elkhound, Pharoah Hound Poodle, Porch Dog, Puli, Shetland Sheepdog, Springer Spaniel, Standard Schnauzer, Toy Poodle, Vizsla, Weimaraner, Welsh Corgi, Wirehaired Pointing Griffon, Yorkshire Tr

Intelligence Index - Cooperation

1

Afghan Hound, Akita, Alaskan Malamute, American Pit Bull or Staffordshire Tr, Beagle, Black and Tan Coonhound, Boxer, Briard, Brussels Griffon, Bulldog, Bullmastiff, Bull Tr, Chow Chow, Giant Schnauzer, Harrier, Jack Russell Tr, Komondor, Lhasa Apso, Old English Sheepdog, Puli, Rottweiler, Miniature Pinscher, Norwegian Elkhound, Norwich Tr, Pekingese, Pomeranian, Rhodesian Ridgeback, Samoyed, Schipperke, Scottish Tr, Siberian Husky, Weimaraner

2

Airedale, Basenji, Basset Hound, Bloodhound, Borzoi, Cairn Tr, Cavalier King Charles Spaniel, Chesapeake Bay Retriever, Chihuahua, Dachshund, Doberman Pinscher, English Setter, Foxhound, Fox Tr, German Pointer, Gordon Setter, Great Dane, Great Pyrenees, Keeshond, Pointer, Porch Dog, Pug, Saint Bernard, Saluki, Scottish Deerhound, Shih Tzu, Silky, Soft-Coated Wheaten Tr, Springer Spaniel, Standard Schnauzer, Tibetan Tr, Whippet, Yorkshire Tr

3

Australian Cattle Dogs, Australian Shepherd, Belgians, Bernese Mountain Dog, Bichon Frise, Border Collie, Border Tr, Brittany Spaniel, Boston Tr, Bouvier des Flandres, Cocker Spaniel, Collie, Dalmatian, German Shepherd, Golden Retriever, Irish Setter, Irish Wolfhound, Italian Greyhound, Japanese Chin, Labrador Retriever, Maltese, Newfoundland, Papillon, Pharoah Hound, Poodle, Shetland Sheepdog, Toy Poodle, Vizsla, Welsh Corgi, West Highland White Tr, Wirehaired Pointing Griffon

www.porchdogs.com

Intelligence Index - Predictability

1

Alaskan Malamute, Australian Shepherd, Basenji, Belgians, Boxer, Brittany Spaniel, Brussels Griffon, Chihuahua, Cocker Spaniel, Dalmatian, Dachshund, Doberman Pinscher, English Setter, Foxhound, Fox Tr, Golden Retriever, Harrier, Irish Setter, Jack Russell Tr, Keeshond, Komondor, Lhasa Apso, Maltese, Miniature Pinscher, Papillon, Pomeranian, Pug, Puli, Saluki, Samoyed, Schipperke, Scottish Tr, Shetland Sheepdog, Toy Poodle, Whippet, Wirehaired Pointing Griffon

2

American Pit Bull or Staffordshire Tr, Basset Hound, Beagle, Bichon Frise, Borzoi, Boston Tr, Cairn Tr, Cavalier King Charles Spaniel, Chesapeake Bay Retriever, Collie, German Shepherd, Giant Schnauzer, Gordon Setter, Italian Greyhound, Japanese Chin, Labrador Retriever, Old English Sheepdog, Pharoah Hound, Poodle, Porch Dog, Rottweiler, Springer Spaniel, Tibetan Tr, Vizsla, Welsh Corgi, Weimaraner, Yorkshire Tr

3

Afghan Hound, Airedale, Akita, Australian Cattle Dog, Bernese Mountain Dog, Black and Tan Coonhound, Bloodhound, Border Collie, Border Tr, Bouvier des Flandres, Briard, Bulldog, Bullmastiff, Bull Tr, Chow Chow, German Pointer, Great Dane, Great Pyranees, Irish Wolfhound, Newfoundland, Norwegian Elkhound, Norwich Tr, Pekingese, Pointer, Rhodesian Ridgeback, Saint Bernard, Scottish Deerhound, Shih Tzu, Siberian Husky, Silky, Soft-Coated Wheaten Tr, Standard Schnauzer, West Highland White Tr

Build

1 | Cavelier King Charles Spaniel, Chihuahua, Italian Greyhound, Japanese Chin, Maltese, Miniature Pinscher, Papillon, Pekingese, Pomeranian, Shih Tzu, Silky Tr, Toy Poodle, Yorkshire Tr

2 | Australian Cattle Dog, Basenji, Beagle, Bichon Frise, Border Tr, Boston Tr, Brittany Spaniel, Brussels Griffon, Cairn Tr, Cocker Spaniel, Dachshund, Fox Tr, Jack Russell Tr, Lhasa Apso, Miniature Pinscher, Porch Dog, Pug, Shetland Sheepdog, Springer Spaniel, Schipperke, Scottish Tr, Shetland Sheepdog, Tibetan Tr, Welsh Corgi, West Highland White Tr

3 | Afghan Hound, Black and Tan Coonhound, Border Collie, Borzoi, Dalmatian, Brittany Spaniel, English Setter, Foxhound, German Pointer, Irish Setter, Pharaoh Hound, Poodle, Porch Dog, Saluki, Scottish Deerhound, Soft-Coated Wheaten Tr, Vizsla, Weimaraner, Whippet

4 | Airdale, Australian Cattle Dog, Australian Shepherd, Basset Hound, Belgians, Bloodhound, Briard, Collie, Foxhound, Golden Retriever, Gordon Setter, Irish Wolfhound, Keeshond, Labrador Retriever, Harrier, Norwegian Elkhound, Pointer, Porch Dog, Puli, Samoyed, Siberian Husky, Standard Schnauzer, Wirehaired Pointing Griffon

5 | Bernese Mountain Dog, Bouvier des Flandres, Bulldog, Chow Chow, Great Pyrenees, Mastiff, Newfoundland, Old English Sheep Dog, Saint Bernard

6 | Akita, Alaskan Malamute, American Pit Bull or Staffordshire Tr, Boxer, Bullmastiff, Chesapeake Bay Retriever, Doberman Pinscher, German Shepherd, Giant Schnauzer, Great Dane, Irish Wolfhound, Komondor, Rhodesian Ridgeback, Rottweiler

Roaming

1 | Airedale, Australian Cattle Dog, Belgians, Bernese Mountain Dog, Bichon Frise, Border Collie, Boxer, Briard, Brittany Spaniel, Bulldog, Cavalier King Charles Spaniel, Chesapeake Bay Retriever, Chihuahua, Chow Chow, Cocker Spaniel, Collie, Dachshund, Doberman Pinscher, English Setter, Great Pyrenees, Irish Setter, Japanese Chin, Keeshond, Lhasa Apso, Newfoundland, Papillon, Pekingese, Pug, Shih Tzu, Silky Tr, Old English Sheepdog, Puli, Saint Bernard, Shetland Sheepdog, Tibetan Terrier, Toy Poodle, Vizsla, Weimaraner, West Highland White Tr, Yorkshire Tr

2 | Afghan Hound, Australian Shepherd, Basset Hound, Border Tr, Borzoi, Boston Tr, Bouvier des Flandres, Brussels Griffon, Bullmastiff, Cairn Tr, Dalmatian, Fox Tr, German Pointer, German Shepherd, Giant Schnauzer, Golden Retriever, Gordon Setter, Great Dane, Irish Wolfhound, Italian Greyhound, Komondor, Labrador Retriever, Maltese, Norwegian Elkhound, Pharoah Hound, Pointer, Pomeranian, Poodle, Porch Dog, Rhodesian Ridgeback, Rottweiler, Samoyed, Schipperke, Scottish Deerhound, Scottish T, Siberian Husky, Springer Spaniel, Standard Schnauz, Welsh Corgi, Whippet, Wirehaired Pointing Griffon

3 | Akita, Alaskan Malamute, American Pit Bull or Staffordshire Tr, Basenji, Beagle, Black and Tan Coonhound, Bloodhound, Foxhound, Harrier, Russell Tr, Miniature Pinscher, Saluki, Soft-Coa Wheaten Tr